Praise for

From her creat

Shoutout to the one and only Laura Dockrill for showing me a world outside my own. *Kemal*

Anyone can teach the theory of writing, but Laura does something unique: with her whimsical charm and her rebellious imagination, she helps you tap into your inner creativity and get beautiful stories on the page. She is a master of gently guiding you to poke and prod at your work at your own pace, all the while preserving the heart of your story. *Jane*

It's not often you find a mentor who helps you find your voice as a writer. Laura helped bring my ideas to life in an authentic and compelling way that was uniquely me. *Ankeeta*

Laura made me realise that writing was something I could take seriously and that my thoughts and ideas would always hold value. Because of Laura, I could dream that one day I'd be sitting where she was, doing the magical thing of telling a room full of kids that I was a writer and that they could be too. *Faye*

Laura taught me that writing is whatever you make it. She is the reason I studied creative writing at university and now work in publishing. Laura is inspirational and I can think of no better person to teach the art of creativity than her. *Sania*

Laura's personal stories are so inspiring, and her writing exercises are encouraging and accessible to all. *Omi*

Also by Laura Dockrill

The Dream House
Big Bones
Aurabel
Lorali

For younger readers
Butterfly Brain

YOU
~*are a*~
STORY

LAURA DOCKRILL

First published in Great Britain in 2023 by
HOT KEY BOOKS
4th Floor, Victoria House
Bloomsbury Square, London WC1B 4DA
Owned by Bonnier Books
Sveavägen 56, Stockholm, Sweden
www.hotkeybooks.com

ISBN: 978-1-4714-1314-8

1

Text design by Louise Millar
Printed and bound in Great Britain by Clays Ltd, Elcograf S.p.A.

Hot Key Books is an imprint of Bonnier Books UK
www.bonnierbooks.co.uk

For
Judith Chamberlain, Gail Bamford, Ms Munroe, Ms Stone, Ms Larnach, Imogen, Stuart, Andrew, Phil, Rachel, Tim, Ms Nelson, Nick Williams, Jill, Dan, Maggie Butt: all inspiring teachers I've met along the way who have flourished my love for creativity and writing, those who made me feel I could; who really didn't have to but did.

Contents

Hello

I have written this book to show you how writing can help with your well-being. I believe writing can improve your mood, give you that fuzzy feeling inside, help you think clearly, calm you down, pleasantly distract you from a bad feeling, showcase your joy, boost your energy or simply give you a reason to hold on. To be proud. To seize the day.

Inside this book are writing exercises that invite you to use memory and emotion as prompts for creating your own material. They are simply invitations. They are doors that you do not have to walk through. You do not have to do anything that makes you feel uncomfortable, unsafe or icky. These exercises are to promote well-being, not impact you negatively. Quite simply, if you are not enjoying the book, put it down. I mean it. It's OK to stop reading if it becomes a chore. A pain or pressure. Or annoying. No thank you. Bye.

Trigger Warning

This book might contain contents that you may find upsetting or distressing. If any of the themes or subject matters do trigger you, ask for help. And please do – asking for help is the best thing I ever did (and still do!). At the back of the book you'll find some resources to support you if you need them.

It should go without saying, but sometimes you do have to state the obvious: everybody is different, every day is different, every circumstance is different. So although writing works for me, it may not work for you, and that is OK! There could be something else that clicks and helps you connect with yourself. So don't take it to heart or be frustrated with yourself if this isn't for you or you don't get the results you wanted. It's my loss but your gain if you go off to find that painting, baking, boxing or learning an instrument does the trick. Whatever works. Do it.

Introduction

My name is Laura, hi, and I have written since I was able to wrap my chubby baby hand round a pencil. I'm not the best at writing. I don't have an impressive vocabulary. I'm not great at spelling and grammar; I get my words in a twist and a tangle. I'm not brilliant at building plots or developing characters – and yet I can't imagine a life without writing. In fact, I feel anxious and weird if I don't write. Like a part of me is missing, unanchored . . . like without it I could come undone. Writing is my touchstone, a family home I keep returning to, like a comfort food, a cosy bed, a base. Writing makes me feel safe.

Writing makes me feel like me.

And I think it could help you feel like you, too. When you and everything around you is changing, and different people want you to be different things at different times, it can be hard to remember who you are. What it feels like to be you, and what it means. It's great to try out different ways of being, but to keep hold of yourself sometimes needs some magic. Writing can be one of those magic tricks, a way of keeping yourself close, a way to remind yourself of who you are and to get to know yourself better – and to love that person too.

That's why I picked up a pen as a child: to process life stuff. To write about how life feels and try to understand it. When my parents broke up. When my heart broke. When my grandma died. When I was scared of moving house. When my feelings felt too big to digest. Writing is a map. A thermometer.

As a child I kept booklets. I was an early riser and would fill my mornings writing and drawing. My dad would handmake notebooks for me before I knew what a notebook even was. They were simple – paper sheets stapled or hole-punched and put together with treasury tags. In these books I would scribble, doodle and scrapbook. I would draw. Collage. Make comics and create stories. Write poems and letters.

As I got older, the notebooks became more 'serious' and personal. Graphs of my growing pains in the form of terrible poetry, and lyrics for my imaginary punk-grunge-rock band that didn't exist (and yet I was the lead singer, of course, even though I couldn't sing. Guys, I would write raps. Can you believe it? Actual RAPS. I mean, what kind of band was this and who did I think I was? Please. Raps that I would read DOWN THE PHONE to the boy I fancied. Raps that would go on for MINUTES. To zero beat). I didn't play football, I couldn't play an instrument, I didn't have the balance for gymnastics, I wasn't into computer games . . . so I wrote: pages and pages of poems, scripts, comics, doodles, letters, scrawls about anything and everything. Let me show you . . .

You're sitting in class. At home your parents are fighting constantly, your bedroom is a mess and you don't have any pocket money. You have outgrown your clothes and you don't have the money to buy the clothes you want to buy to look cool. You fancy someone who doesn't love you back and isn't quite, unsurprisingly, ready to run away and have babies with you yet. Which is perfect for you because you still haven't kissed anyone and that's terrifying for you also. Your best friend has been sitting next to somebody else at lunchtime, and you've heard they're going to the cinema this weekend and they haven't invited you because the film is rated 18 and you're a goody-goody two shoes and so you just won't get it. The feeling makes your belly lurch. Makes your hairs stand up. Stings and prickles your cheeks like you've been slapped. Slapped round the heart. School's not for you. Maybe you don't get what the teacher is even on about right now. It's all going over your head. You feel stupid. You feel alone. You see adverts with other kids your age in them and they are glossy and smiley and happy and eating crunchy cereal and going off to school with a bright red backpack. Why can't you be like that? What is wrong with you? You cringe at the past; you're scared of the future. You worry about your existence. About death. You're unhappy with your body. And it's changing. Gross.

You're like a time bomb, waiting to explode. You're unhappy with your hair. Why is it always greasy? You hate your dumpy school shoes. You took the risk of scuffing them up in the hope your parents would notice and agree to buy you a fresh pair that you can actually stand but they don't, and now you've got ugly AND scuffed-up shoes. And you're dreading exams and the long walk where you're scared of seeing the mean kids from that other school again who once threw chips at you and laughed at you all the way home. Home, where there aren't even any good snacks.

What do you do? You write about it. You write. You write until your fingers hurt. Until the paper burns. Write until your eyes blur and your words spin and the stories fly. You write your heart into a new rhythm. You write to the time of your pulse. You write your belly into butterflies. You write yourself to sleep.

I would often fall asleep mid-writing, with notebooks at the end of my bed like a frenzied FBI agent trying to solve a mystery. I was trying to crack a case. What was this all about? Why was I even here?

(Spoiler alert: the case is still unsolved.)

But you don't stop, you never stop; you write yourself into tomorrow. Until the next day and the day after that.

Look, you might not see yourself as a great writer – you might not even think of yourself as a writer at all! But I still think this book is for you. You might have picked this book up because you love to write. Me too. You might have picked this book up because you love to read – well, me too. You might just love words. The way they sound. The way they look on the page. You might not have any reason at all for opening up this book and yet here we are. You might have been given this book from a friend. Or maybe your old Nana Doris got it for you for Christmas. Oh, hey, Nana Doris, who didn't know what else to get you and you're like, oh, cheers, great, thanks a lot. I would have preferred the socks. You might be like, you don't know me at all. Thanks but no thanks – writing is NOT for me. Books are for losers, man. Stories are dry.

Even though you yourself are a story.

You might have picked up this book because you've been working on a piece of writing in your spare time, a massive epic adventure story, and want to flex. Maybe you're trying to brush up on your writing techniques? Maybe you've always wanted to write? Or maybe it's your story? Maybe you feel like your mood has been a bit flat recently and you don't know why; you want to take care of yourself and are trying new things? Maybe you need to let it all out, express yourself? Find clarity? Maybe it's the opposite – you want to take your mind off it all, and just have fun and play. Maybe you're just looking for ways to busy yourself and find a hobby? Maybe you're thinking of starting a journal or diary? Maybe you're just exploring your creativity? Maybe you just . . . want to write? To pick a pen up like you did when you were a child? Before you cared what people thought. Maybe you want to tell a story and don't know how or where to begin? Maybe you're just thinking . . . why not?

Maybe you feel like a bottle of fizzy drink about to explode? You need to release. Maybe you haven't listened to yourself for a long time and that chat is long overdue? Maybe you're in pieces, or going through something tough. Maybe somebody you love is. Maybe you've always lived alongside something difficult or are apprehensive about something ahead? Maybe you're trying to unpick a knot in your mind?

Maybe you're trying to write yourself out of something hard?

Well, if you are, for that I am sorry.

But the really good news is that there are things you can do to comfort yourself along the way.

And if you're going that way anyway . . . you may as well write about it, right?

About this book and how to use it

Try, have a go, let's see what comes . . .

As much as I love words and believe in the healing power of shared stories, I get it: no writing journal is going to be a full-blown bonfire torching up your soul into the blissful heights of a pain-free existence and give you an easy life.

But let this book be a little lantern, a warm glow, to sit with you whatever you're going through. The exercises in this book will help you capture your feelings and tell your stories in your very own voice.

This book belongs to you. It is not mine; you are completely in control. If the exercises feel too heavy, tone them down. Too light? Turn them up. They are only starting points. Seeds for your forest. Go and grow a jungle of words! Use the exercises that work for you. If they don't connect, no sweat – move on to the next one and ignore me completely. Feel free to adapt, take bits you like, cross me out and make notes. You know what you need. There are no rules. There are no rights or wrongs. There are no answers. There is no good or bad. You could read the book through from start to finish. You could dip in somewhere and out somewhere else. You could have a flick through and create your own exercises or apply the tools to something else, like art or music. It's your ride.

And yes, I know, it's quite audacious to write a book on writing. Especially as I don't have all the answers. You might be dubious, I get that. In case you're worried that I'm some fraudster con artist: as well as writing for myself, I have taught creative writing for over ten years in various forms to all ages, in and out of the UK. That said, through teaching I have learned A LOT more than I've taught. And I'm still learning too. However, some things, like writing, you cannot simply teach – but you can hold spaces for it to happen and you can hold hands along the way too. You can't hear or see me saying the words next to you, but know that I am here! And I am not the 'teacher'. We are doing this side by side.

Anybody is welcome to use this book. (Well, everybody except the negative voice of self-criticism who – sorry, you aren't welcome here, mate, access denied.) If you're young, EVEN BETTER – you will have a head start to a healthy head! You are helping yourself by beginning.

One

WHY WRITE?

'I write because it helps me to understand the world and myself a little better.'

NIKESH SHUKLA

We all have our own reasons for writing. Have you ever thought about why you write? Or are thinking about writing? Maybe it's an invisible pull that you can't even put into words. Writing can help us express ourselves, process our thoughts, break down big feelings, communicate, connect, digest and make sense of ourselves and others. That doesn't mean the writing itself has to make sense. Maybe you don't know the reason you want to write, and you really don't need one either. What is important is that you write for you.

Other than writing for a career, here are some reasons people might pick up a pen:

Connection.

Fun.

Freedom.

Activism.

To entertain.

Escape.

Silence.

Release.

Peace.

Praise.

Proof they exist.

Curiosity.

Acceptance.

Growth.

Change.

Exploration.

Discovery.

Understanding.

To be heard.

Driven by an emotion or feeling.

Avoidance.

Desire.

Urge.

Ambition.
Relief.
Forgiveness.
Spirituality.
Meditation.
Expression.
Distraction.
Boredom.
Comfort.
Company.

To problem-solve.
To process.
To digest.
To push boundaries.
To challenge.
To cleanse.
Reinvention.
Role play.
To tell the truth.
To feel better.

Author Clover Stroud says she creates things that help her **'communicate what life feels like'**.

Novelist Haruki Murakami says, **'I have only one reason to write novels, and that is to bring the dignity of the individual soul to the surface and shine a light upon it.'**

Poet and novelist Salena Godden says when she began her novel *Mrs Death Misses Death* she was **'in a very dark place and looking for the light'**.

Poet Lemn Sissay says that **'Poetry is the voice at the back of the mind. I write to express and interpret the world around me through that voice.'**

This sounds like the 'writers' of the world are doing it for us. But, look, Hilary Mantel describes writing as **'running in the imagination'**, which I just love. I'd quite like to get breathless on the page. I'd like to see where my words take me. It makes writing feel alive. In the same way that fancying a jog around the park doesn't mean you have to enter the Olympics, journaling before bed doesn't mean you have to write 100,000 words and go on to win the Booker Prize.

You can just do this for you. Quiet. Cosy. In your own place at your own pace.

Nobody has to know, ever.

Writing is NOT a competitive sport.

And please don't fret that writing here will use your writing energies up. Creativity doesn't get used up like a jar of peanut butter and sorry all shops have run out of peanut butter for ever and the factory is closed. Creativity breeds creativity. If anything, to create creates more.

When you create, you can feel it. Others will too. Once you begin making, you will be noticeably zingy, electric, bright, light and sparky to hang around with. You will have a glow.

So why do I write?

As you know, I have never not written. I don't know a life without writing. I have written for fun. For my job. For expression. For freedom. For joy.

Until that pen of mine became more than just ink – it became a life jacket . . .

Whatever your difficult stuff is – and I will explain mine in a bit – it is only by living it that we can begin to understand it. I am not saying that writing about difficult stuff will overnight magic you better or fix a situation. And I am definitely not saying that writing or creativity is medicine by itself. But writing about it *alongside* it, for me, became the only option. I wrote like my life depended on it, boy. And when I wrote, I felt like

I was setting myself free. I learned that trying to run from the unknown only made me more afraid of it. I learned to lean into the unknown; I practised making myself comfortable in the discomfort. And so I wrote. It didn't have to be good and it didn't have to make sense.

I write to remind myself of me

My writing voice is my friend. I know it might sound silly, but to neglect her means I'm not listening to myself. My writing is that girl who pops her head round the door and says 'Guess what?' She holds my hand, tells me jokes and stories. She holds me close and says, 'Together we can do this. I'm with you, as I always have been. You are not alone.'

I write to release feelings

When I was going through a difficult time, there were lots of things I felt I couldn't or shouldn't say out loud. And yet on the page, on my phone or typed up, I felt I could get everything off my chest and that made me feel better. On the page I could tell the truth, repeat myself as many times as I needed, swear, rant and rage! I also felt that after writing I was better to be around – lighter – and that I had the capacity to be there for my loved ones because I had done something for myself.

I write to remember things

Writing is also INCREDIBLE for memory. When I was revising for exams at school (hmmm, not that often, but when it did happen) information went into my brain quicker and clearer if I wrote down what I was learning. Writing can help us locate memories, process events and make some sense of the messy blur of life.

I write down MY version of the story

Writing my truth down about the bad things that happened felt like mining my way through the pain to tunnel myself out of the darkness. Writing was evidence. It gave me a clearer understanding, a narrative that put my events in order. Perspective. And eventually that was very powerful; it helped me draw a line, accept and make peace with the past.

I write to escape

Writing was a welcome escape. We can't always drop everything and run away to a remote beach (even if we could afford to). But with a pen, even just for fifteen minutes, I was able to escape and distract myself. I was boundless and free. Writing can be a welcome distraction.

To work through an issue

Even just the very act of writing made me feel like I was doing something to actively problem-solve, to at least try to feel better. It also allowed me to track my feelings and see how far I'd come so I could look back at my recovery. This gave me agency, control and even a tiny particle of power. I saw writing like de-knotting a bunch of tangled-up fairy lights that have been stored in the dusty attic of my head.

One day I would be able to plug myself in and – AHHHHHHH!!! – now we have light.

To connect

Storytelling is all about connection. It is an agreement between the teller and the listener – even if that listener is simply the paper you are writing on, the walls of your bedroom that look on as you write, your cat snoozing by your feet or the almighty wind. It is still a contract, a promise of some kind, saying, 'I care and I'll always be here'. It is about trust.

Listening is so important. In fact, it's something I'm still trying to get better at; it is a skill. Listen, listen, listen. And to listen well, actively, is a gift! And it takes practice. But one of the things that really helped me get better was sharing: sharing my story and listening to others'.

Listening to other people's stories inspired me to do the same, encouraged me to tell my experience, allowed me to talk. Helped me to know that I wasn't alone.

I feel connected, empathetic, kinder, more patient, more understanding and understood. And without story, without experience, what is life?

And so, writing made me see that I am grateful for my difficult experiences. It has changed me for the better.

Sur-thrive-al

Us humans are designed to survive. It's our instinct. It's our calling. It's our sole purpose: to exist. SURVIVE, kid, that's all you have to do. And when you are experiencing something challenging or difficult all you WANT to do, all you maybe CAN do, is drag your animal body through it. All you want is to eat again, sleep again, be yourself again . . .

When you overcome something challenging or difficult, phew, you've got two options.

Option One: you can go on with your life and move forward. That's great, absolutely WELL DONE YOU!

Or Option Two: you can USE all that stuff. All that pain and heartbreak, all that loss, sadness, upset and grief, the confusion and complication – to your advantage; you can learn from it, grow from it, thrive from it. Make it YOURS. OWN it, celebrate yourself and what you've done. You can talk about it, write about it, help others with it and throw yourself into the light. (This does not mean you have to share it.)

A word on mindfulness

A lot of this might sound like or remind you of 'mindfulness'. A lot of the writing process is mindfulness, naturally. You write to clear your head; it can be calming and relaxing, cathartic and cleansing. But sometimes it is HEAVY, HARD WORK. Something that is mentally and physically exhausting. I sometimes find writing to be quite aerobic! I mean it, sometimes I actually sweat (more on that, oh don't you worry).

I struggle with the word 'mindfulness'. I find prescriptive mindfulness does the opposite for me. It feels unnatural to be sitting there in silence, being still with my thoughts bumbling their way around my head, boxing my brains in. Forcing myself to lie down quietly when I felt I should be doing something, being somewhere. Sometimes, when I was in recovery, mindfulness felt like being locked in on a private candlelit dinner date with my mental illness – oh, cooey, no thank you.

So writing, for me, is a perfect way of combining mindfulness with doing – rather than sitting and waiting to get better I was processing while writing. When I wrote, I felt like I was filing my thoughts and feelings. I was basically becoming my own therapist, talking it through, hashing it out, throwing it around.

Writing it to death, basically.

Mindfulness simply means being in the present, in the moment, doing something for you that is beneficial to your well-being. And writing is just that.

So why should you write?

Everybody can write. EVERYBODY. You don't need writing experience. You don't need qualifications, an elaborate vocabulary, A-star grammar or a fancy desk. All you need is a brain and a heart to write the guts out of something. And it doesn't have to be perfect. But it has to be you.

Here are some truths about writing and why it is the most perfect hobby to take up.

The time is now

You can never be too young or too old to begin.

You don't need anything to get started

You don't need a ridiculous feathered quill or a brand-new shiny MacBook or even a brand-new expensive notebook (although that is a nice feeling). You don't need excuses. You don't need peace and quiet or a break-the-bank fancy chair. You just need your brain and your heart.

It's free

Writing costs nothing. Financially it can be pencil-and-notebook cheap if you want it to be. The only thing writing potentially costs is your time, and there are worse ways to spend your precious time. If you aren't quite in the headspace to get that mammoth twelve-part fantasy draft down just yet, there are exercises in this book as short as a minute. Even five minutes a day is enough to improve your writing muscles, reboot your flow and recharge you.

You can pick it up and put it down

Writing works around you. You can pick it up at any point in your life and then put it back down again – it flows in that way. You don't have to prepare anything. It is a jack-in-a-box art form that springs to life on your command. Leave it for a while and it's like riding a bike: you'll always remember how to do it. Write every day, however, and it's your secret superpower, your gift.

You can take it with you anywhere

I've got nothing against the double bass or a surfboard, but could you imagine carting those things around the world? Writing is the most lightweight, compact hobby that can live in your pocket if you choose.

You don't have to prove yourself

You don't need a cover letter listing a thousand reasons why you should begin writing. Writing has no grade system. You don't have to audition. You just show up.

You don't even need to have anything to write about

This is not a trauma contest! You don't need a gritty subject matter or to have experienced something dark and harrowing. This can be light and easy-breezy too. See what comes and there is beauty and wonder to be found in the everyday and in our imaginations.

It hurts nobody

Writing is not a bloodsport.

It is a conversation but . . . with yourself.

It is a form of communication but . . . it is silent.

It is a form of communion but . . . nobody else has to be there.

You can be loud on the page. You can shout. You can scream. You can swear.

You are working, you are sharing and you are healing, and you are doing it all from the inside out in the privacy of your own space. You never have to show your work to a single soul. It belongs completely to you. You hold the pen.

It belongs to you

We touch on sharing and ownership of work later on, but know that all your writing belongs to you. It is YOURS. This is really important. When you're young it's not always easy to find anything that is sacred. When I was growing up I shared a bedroom with my sister – once she was tired the light had to go off, so that stopped my writing! If I wanted to sit in a library to write I'd have to ask permission from my parents. If I wanted to sit in a cafe, I had to ask for money from my parents for a cup of tea. Growing up is full of compromise, conditions, repecussions, sharing and asking – but not here on the page. No, this is yours, so let the page be your home – and you can decorate it how you like.

It can help

Writing wasn't the only thing that got me well, but it was a big one. I returned to the page how a yogi does a yoga mat. My writing book became my sanctuary. Telling my story unzipped my armour and allowed me to be myself.

You don't need to worry about . . .

Spelling and grammar. Word count. Deadlines or what anybody will think. Don't even worry about the quality of the writing itself, please. This not about being judgemental, competitive, self-critical or a martyr – that's unhelpful and gets in the way. This is about being kind to ourselves. This is about holding ourselves close. Getting a feeling across, not a spelling test. YUCK.

You can do as much or as little as you like. The exercises in this book are only prompts to get you going, so do with them as you wish! This is not an exam. This is unjudgemental, free-spirited, boundless, unadulterated, triumphant real talk!

What you might need

For your headspace, privacy and clarity, you might want to get yourself a notebook (nothing fancy) or folder (an actual physical folder or on your desktop) to keep everything together. Keep it somewhere safe and close and easy to find.

You can write by hand or on a device and on or with anything. I actually wrote my memoir (more about this later) on my phone! You don't get marked down for not writing your love poems on a typewriter. If you don't have access to writing material or are unable to write manually, you can record your voice, write in your mind, whisper your words or bloody sing them from the rooftops. You could wear a pair of satin pyjamas and ask your little brother to type them up for you as you recite your wordy descriptions from a velvet chaise longue while eating a box of truffles. I don't care how, just **Get. It. Done.**

If you find writing about yourself as yourself too uncomfortable or gross or weird or upsetting, there are exercises in this book in which you can disguise, conceal and ribbon your personal thoughts and feelings. Trust me, it's how most writers write.

What happened to me

How could I expect you to feel safe writing your experience without sharing mine? I'll let you in on why I can truly say that writing down what happened to me saved my life.

In 2018 I was hit with a severe and rare mental illness called post-partum psychosis. The illness was triggered by the birth of my son – yes, the most natural thing in the world, childbirth. I had experienced a healthy 'normal' pregnancy and have no history of mental illness. I had no idea anybody could get so mentally unwell after something as primal as having a baby.

The illness's symptoms came on hard and fast and were cruel and extreme. I experienced delusions, insomnia, racing thoughts, paranoia, mania, intrusive thoughts, depression, anxiety and suicidal thoughts. (Sounds dreamy, right?)

I mean, I couldn't even eat! And I can always eat.

As you can imagine, it wasn't what I pictured

having my first baby would look like. It's just not something they show in the movies and books when you're meant to be the 'happiest' you've ever felt.

The illness left me scared. Confused. Alone. Desperate. Stalked by shame and guilt and totally heartbroken. Completely lost and out of my depth. Rock-bottom. With self-esteem below zero. Every day felt like weightlifting, climbing a mountain, fighting a fire. I believed I would never recover, that the illness would swallow me whole, that I'd never make it out alive. That I would never live to tell the tale . . .

And then I did the best thing I could have possibly done. I asked for help. This is the bit I'm most proud of. Because it takes a lot of courage to say you can't cope, that you can't manage, that you're scared of something nobody else can see or hear or feel or know or understand.

It got worse before it got better, but asking for help got me on my path of recovery. And for the first time I felt relief. I began to see a faint light at the end of the dark tunnel.

My recovery wasn't linear – it was bumpy, boy. I was like a moth at a light bulb, trying, hoping that each day I'd wake up and feel a little better.

I wanted to draw a line under it all and pretend it had never happened. The last thing I wanted to do was relive it. I didn't want to think about it or talk about it. I didn't want it to define me, shape me, bruise me; I didn't want it to change me. I wanted my personality back. I wanted to feel happy. To be able to eat my dinner in peace. To laugh like I used to. I just wanted to wear my nice clothes and do lovely things – play with my little boy, go back to writing stories, see my friends, read a book, dance to music, cook yummy food. To say 'I'm good' and actually mean it. To feel 'normal'.

I felt that writing it all down would be like kicking a wasps' nest.

Whereas I used to believe my imagination was my superpower, I was now afraid of it because it had turned on me and stabbed me in the back. I no longer trusted my mind – it wasn't that safe space I ran off to dream in; it was no longer my escape. It was an enemy. My psychosis knew all my weak spots and had used them against me! Plus, I felt like a zombie too. I had no energy and couldn't concentrate I truly believed that my mental illness had robbed my creativity, inspiration and instinct.

I painted a smile on and said out loud that I was 'doing great'. But it was a lie. I threw away the clothes I had worn when I was sick, moved the furniture around. End of story. Goodbye. But hard stuff and painful memories and experience don't always work like that. You can't run or hide from them. They always get you in the end . . .

What could I do?

One day, a bit like prodding a sore ulcer with my tongue, I found my story was bubbling to the surface, erupting, like an overflowing pan of boiling pasta. I couldn't keep this inside for ever. And so I began to write. But very slowly and very gently, bit by bit. I tried to jot down just a little about what had happened, a few words here and there. There was no secret – I just began to write.

Where did I start? The beginning, I suppose.

And then I'd stop . . . and check for the monster. Is it coming back?

The words added up into sentences, into lines, into pages . . . and once I started I couldn't stop. I ended up writing 275,000 words in just three months. With a newborn on my chest.

And afterwards . . . well, I felt a hell of a lot better to be honest.

For the first time in months I felt like I could breathe. Like I had removed about seventeen layers of unwanted clothing. I felt free. I felt liberated.

I felt really brave. I felt really, truly proud of myself. These were also feelings I hadn't felt in a very long time. And then I started to see the illness differently. My perspective had changed because I had processed it and altered my view; I saw what I had overcome and felt MORE proud.

But even better than that: I was no longer afraid. I felt in control. I had insight. I realised I was a warrior (just wearing an oversized pink jumper and my sister's cupcake socks instead of armour). And the monster seemed to not dissolve exactly, but fall asleep next to me. In fact, the monster almost began to protect me. It reminded me how far I'd come. I began to accept that monster of mine.

And then that gave me the courage to share my writing and that was even better. Because then guess what happened? Other stories came back to me. And hearing and sharing stories only helped to colour in my recovery even more. Then I felt part of something greater – something universal. And that reassured me and comforted me. I felt like I had written myself out of something difficult. And that empowered me.

Every time I get a positive reaction from my experience, I feel lifted. I feel less scared of my illness. I feel like the experience gets filed in my brain under 'NOT SO GREAT BUT IT WAS MANAGEABLE' rather than 'ARGHHHHHHHH!

THAT WAS AWFUL'. And that, for me, means I am more likely to move forward with my life without the fear of it coming back.

I realised that I'd always written myself out of difficult challenges. That I'd always transformed my pain and joy into my work. That my pen has always been my friend. My passport. My therapy. My holiday. My medicine. My adventure. My time-travelling machine. My filing cabinet. My identity. My diary. My home. My heart.

Two

WARMING UP TO WRITING

Clear your head and warm up your imagination.

Making the first mark is probably the hardest part of all. It comes with expectation, pressure, doubt and worry. Here comes the inner critic – what if it's rubbish? It could also be frightening thinking about what will come out . . .

It takes a lot of courage, intelligence and wisdom to part with your thoughts. We worry that once the actual physical letters are down on a page or screen that they become a fact. That you have to march this very second to some back alley and get those words tattooed on your forehead. That your words are irreversible and that you have to stand by them for ever. But think about how a painter will often sketch vignettes before committing. How any great chef's famous recipe comes from years of experimentation, from improvement and practice. See your creation as clay. Fluid. Flexible. Evergreen and slinky. Allow yourself to move with it. Adapt. The first words you write are probably not going to end up being the opening scene to your Oscar-winning film (they might, but there will most likely be many, many drafts in between). Don't let yourself be bullied by the fresh newness of a piece of paper!

But do be excited!

Wear in your notebook – make the first mark

Having a new notebook can be like owning a pair of box-fresh white trainers. You don't want to get them dirty so you watch your every step and might not have as much fun or adventure than if you were wearing old boots.

Don't miss out. I say, break the seal! Fill your first writing page with whatever comes. Scribble, scratch, make marks, play. Rip it up, tear it out, do a drawing, write a poem. Make a coffee ring. Do not let your notebook pressurise or bluff you into thinking the line you are about to write has got to be immediate poetry. Make your first page be the page you care for the least. Decorate your writing book, love it, hold it, carry it around with you, wear it in, make it yours.

There is no such thing as bad writing. It doesn't exist. I will be here the whole time – this little lamp, this warm glow – to light your fire, to keep your words burning. You are not alone.

Some things to remember

Here are some pointers to have in mind when you're writing, to help keep the material truthful, original and impactful. Remember: don't be afraid to find the confidence to sound like yourself.

Write what you know

Only you know what it's like being you. What it's like sitting in your room in your home. Only you know what you eat for breakfast. What you dream of. What you're scared of. What makes you happy. What you love. This is all gold dust. When you're a writer, everything is important. Everything counts. The more personal, the more truthful, the more detailed, the more silly, the better. This does not mean you have to give everything away to a reader but dig deep and draw upon everything you know to tell your story and create new ones. You are important. There is only one you. You have something to say. It's about getting to the root.

Deep, deep down . . .

Anybody can write the bones of a story.

You write the soul.

Ernest Hemingway said, **'Write hard and clear about what hurts.'** Nobody can write your story better than you. It is so clichéd. But it's so true. The one book out of the fifteen that I have published that has translated the most, which I still receive the greatest number of messages and feedback from, has been my memoir, *What Have I Done?*, a book about something that really happened to me. To write it I didn't have to invent a plot, I didn't have to write a plan, I didn't have to add twists and turns, I didn't have to build new characters or amplify the drama. I didn't mess around with tense or form or genre. It was about my life and **I just wrote**.

Me and a pen and nothing in between.

And, yes, the entire time the inner critic was present. And fear. Whispering in the background, 'Nobody cares. Nobody is ever going to read this. This is terrible, Laura. You can't write. Why are you so annoying?' But I kept going. I had to.

Telling that story has given me back so much more than what the illness took from me. It's all there in those pages – I only have to see it to remind myself how far I've come. I see it almost like a work of fiction now. It's difficult to imagine I was the girl inside that book.

That's how powerful storytelling can be.

AHHHHH, NOW EVERYONE KNOWS MY SECRETS

If you're conscious that writing in your own voice is too revealing or exposing for even you, or maybe you're anxious that someone will find and read your work (HOW VERY DARE THEY?), there are ways to disguise and protect yourself.

You could play with tenses. You could write about yourself from second person (i.e., you pick up a pen, you write down your thoughts) or third person (i.e., they pick up a pen, they write their thoughts down) or experiment with voice.

You could use the voice of a made-up character (the lead characters of many fiction writers are usually just themselves with a new name!).

You could create a new code or language of your own.

You could bury your real thoughts into fiction. Say what you want to say, but build a new world around you. You could set your scenes in the past, in fantasy or another location. Change times, dates, appearances. Who would you be in another life?

Don't overdo the homework

Writing what you know doesn't mean you can't write about what you don't. Like the past or places you haven't been, or that don't even exist. That's the cool thing about writing: there are no rules. You could take your modern-day love story or the description of your breakfast and place it in the past – remember, it's the feeling we're trying to get across, not the accuracies.

When it comes to researching, don't overdo it (unless you are writing non-fiction or biography and it needs to be backed up). A reader just wants a hint of place, signposts, an aroma. Don't overwhelm your reader (or yourself) with fussy facts and dates. This is all just extra stuff that can be important for the writer to know but not the reader.

Have a peep down the rabbit hole but don't fall in entirely and get lost. This is not a history or geography class. We still want you grounded. We still want your voice.

The beauty of daydreaming

At school we are taught to concentrate. We've all seen films where a kid is wistfully gazing out of the window and the history teacher will snap them out of it, asking them to answer a painfully hard question on the spot. Yes, sir, it's important to focus, but LET ME LIVE. Let's look through the lens of happiness for a minute and see that daydreaming is wonderful, essential, natural, healthy and important. And in the bubbling world of writing, daydreaming is a friend, a much-loved visitor. So dream, dream, dream. Give yourself permission. So long as it isn't harmful and you aren't disturbing yourself, go for it! It's a great skill to be able to fly off into the depths and heights of your imagination – that's what it's for! For living out fantasies, passing the time on trains or in queues at the shops. Daydreaming is writing in your head, don't let anybody tell you otherwise!

Imposter syndrome

WHOA there . . . HOLD ON, you might be thinking, I'm not even a good writer! What if what I write is rubbish? What if it's terrible? What if it's so bad it makes me feel worse?

All these doubts are completely 'normal'. It only means you care. And nobody wants a cocky smug buffoon roaming around the place boasting to everyone about how good they are at everything the entire time. That said, we might need a little bit of that confidence to get going. To give ourselves a chance. How do we know unless we try? Writing is about curiosity and exploration – no pressure, no strain, no stress. See it as an experiment. Not a judgement.

I have doubts at least once a day that I'm rubbish at writing. I always think I'm not clever enough, quick enough, funny, successful, cool, talented, wise enough – the list goes on. Not to be all inspirational quote about it but GET OUT OF YOUR WAY and see what happens then.

ALL writers suffer with imposter syndrome; it's a part of the job. All adults probably suffer with it – they just pretend they don't. I think it's endearing to admit it; it shows vulnerability and care.

We cover the inner critic later on too.

Vulnerability is a super-strength NOT a weakness.

I would also argue that no writing is 'good' or 'bad' (I mean, I could ask you what even IS good or bad? – but that's a whole other book). If what you've written is true, as in it's come from your heart and brain and you mean the words on the page, then it's the truth, the whole truth and nothing BUT. It's your truth. If your words sound like you, look like you, stink of you, then they are YOU.

Who can argue with your truth? Who can tell you, you are anything other than yourself?

This is greater than 'good' or 'bad' . . .

This just IS!

Who cares?

Someone will. Trust me. Even if that someone is you. I've learned that the experiences we think are most personal are actually the most universal. If you were to set your work free into the world you might change somebody's life . . . You might save somebody's life. But don't worry about that for now.

For now this isn't about them.

This is about YOU.

You just write – write for you. Write what you wish you could have read when you were in the thick of something. Write what you want to read if you were to ever experience something challenging. Write something you wish you could give to your younger self or your future self.

Or, better still, just write.

And if you happen to end up helping someone else while you're at it, then YES PLEASE!

Warming up

It is not advisable to run a marathon without warming up – to get the blood flowing, the muscles stretched and activated. But also, our brain is the boss, right? If I ever give up on a run (er, almost every time, LOL) it's because my head has told me to stop, not my legs. So it's the brain we're taking care of, and warming it up sends signals to the rest of our body that we are about to use it.

Writing is the same. Especially if we haven't written creatively for a while (or ever).

So here is the secret to the formidable invisible six-pack that is my brain: these warm-up exercises. They are little bursts of writing you can do to keep your head clear, your heart cleansed, your soul fed and your imagination muscles warm. They are short and they pack a punch. All these can be done on the go and they are a great way to keep up writing when you haven't got all the time in the world. They are also great for starting a new project and refocusing, so you can come back to them over and over.

As well as warming up your brain, these exercises help you create something special. We are trying to play around with our thoughts and memories to unlock something, to jostle a stone and overturn something; we are almost trying to get ourselves into the habit of writing while at the same time break out of the habit of routine thinking.

Morning notes

It's tempting to pick up your phone as soon as you've snapped your eyes open. Something you could do instead or alongside, in your notebook or in even in your phone, is at the very start of your day, as soon as you've woken up, ask yourself, quite simply:

How am I?

or

How are you?

If that feels too direct, you could try:

How are things?

And see what happens.

You could try the same before bed too.

Don't worry about it making sense or being neat and tidy.

You don't have to do anything with these notes. You could see them as simply a way to energise or unwind and recyle them straight away. But you could use them to track your day or log your mood. Perhaps to see, even, if your mood has changed since you've introduced the tiniest bit of regular writing into your routine.

Be honest with yourself

Yes, these exercises are light, but they still matter. If you find it hard to be honest with yourself, you might find it a little easier to face things on the page.

What's on your mind? Have you got a thought on a loop? Maybe you've had a weird conversation with a friend recently that's left you fizzing? Maybe you're worried you said the wrong thing? You're fearful that you've upset someone or are slipping behind at school? Maybe you have bigger worries going on? About home, a family member or about the world? Your future? Are you looking forward to something? Maybe there's someone you like? Maybe you're experiencing feelings that you've never had before and you're not sure what to do with them? Where do those feelings go? Maybe you can feel a change coming . . .

This is your chance to dump it! To let it all out. You might find that writing it all down releases you, makes you feel lighter or helps you to process.

A shoebox

Have you ever woken up after the wildest dream and gone, 'Wow, that could have been a film', only to tell it to somebody, who looks at you utterly confused, like you're completely mad – and then you regret ever even opening your mouth? I know that feeling only too well. If only we could film our dreams to show somebody what we created! Dreams are so inspiring and can produce some really juicy stuff. So, rather than put any of my loved ones through the pain of pretending to be interested in my dreams, I began to write them down.

I used to keep a shoebox under my bed. It was big and pink. Inside I kept a stack of paper and a pen. I've always had very dramatic vivid dreams, and I can usually remember them. Every morning when I woke up, the first thing I did, sometimes without even opening my eyes, was reach my hand down and yank open the box. Then I'd write down the dream from the night before. Exactly as it was. I didn't think about it, I just did it. I wanted to capture it as raw and as pure as I could get it, with all the feelings and energy. The strange thing was it was like my brain started to catch on to the fact that I was writing my dreams down and in turn they became more elaborate. More theatrical, MORE wild.

When I have strange dreams I sometimes look them up on dream-analysing websites – I don't believe in much of that and I'm not superstitious, but they can throw up some really interesting themes, offer ideas, fascinating perspectives and shed new light. It's a fun way to make new characters, storylines and plots. So you might want to hold on to those morning notes as future inspiration rather than throwing them away!

Free writing

Free writing is a spring clean for the head. It's like clearing the surface before you begin cooking, setting the table before eating a lovely meal or, quite simply, turning over a fresh page. I learned how to free-write during my creative writing degree. I say 'learned how', but there isn't a way to write, and there certainly isn't a way to write freely – otherwise that surely defeats the object. This type of writing as an exercise can be helpful to encourage you to ignore perfectionism, and get stuff down.

I recommend free writing with paper and pen so it's nice and loose (but do whatever works for you), and timing yourself. (It can be fun on your phone but sometimes autocorrect can get in the way . . . which can be fun too!)

THE RULES:

- Write whatever comes into your head.
- It can be random words, a list. No punctuation needed or even complete sentences.
- Yes, you can invent new words.
- Try not to think about what you are writing.
- Try not to censor yourself.
- Don't worry about spelling or grammar.
- Don't worry about handwriting.
- Don't worry about repetition.

- Be as honest as you can. Go with the thoughts that come.
- Nobody has to read this, ever. You can EAT the paper when you are finished if you choose to.
- You cannot stop until your time is up.
- No theme.

Set the timer for five minutes.
GO!

By the way, it took several sessions for me to not just see the exercise as kind of pointless. I would repeat myself and find it really difficult not to see my flaws, fight the urge to correct and read back over everything to make it 'perfect'. But when this exercise works effectively I feel like I am almost in a meditative state, with my heart leading my hand. It is the closest I get to 'listening' to myself.
And that is when writing comes – proper writing. And I feel I can go for pages and pages. I always come away from free writing with a tasty writer's bump on my finger big enough to serve as a perch for a parrot. And I feel PROUD. OK, this doesn't mean that anybody else would ever want to read what I've written! And why should they? This writing belongs to me, as yours does to you.

I don't think I've ever shared my free writing with anybody, but that doesn't mean it doesn't generate ideas, because it really does. It brings up a lot!

Also, because it is so fast-paced it can be a great way of exorcising heavy stuff and clearing skeletons out of the cupboard without overthinking what you are getting down.

Focused free writing

This is the same technique, using the same rules as for free writing, but this time we are free writing to a theme. These are all brilliant ways to begin, and even if they sound generic and simple, your answers might surprise you. Try to go with the first one that sticks out instinctively to you. Set a timer for a couple of minutes and try free writing on personal experience to these themes . . .

A holiday
A birthday
A friend
A dream
A crush
An item of clothing
A pair of shoes
A pet/animal
A job/chore
A gift

You could keep going for ever . . . You could then develop the themes so they get a little juicier and deeper to challenge your thoughts a bit more.

Here are some to try . . .

Something that changed you

Something you want/ed

A regret

Something that didn't go as you expected

Something that makes you happy

Somebody you love

Somebody who loves you

A time you said sorry

A time somebody said sorry to you

An object of significance

Roulette

This is an easy way to get loads written down. Take some words from a book on your shelf – maybe a dictionary or a novel. You could choose words from text messages, the TV or radio, or ask friends and family to throw some new words at you. Blend everyday words with elaborate ones. With any words you don't know the meaning of, try to guess before you find out. Write all your roulette words down in a list, or you could fill a box or bag with them on scraps of paper and pull them out one at a time like Scrabble letters. This could be a collection of words you return to, favourite words that you build up over time.

Here are some words that I've taken from books on my shelf:

Insect
Wheel
Teeth
Sky
Water
Electricity
Claw
Window
Stool

Beam
Glass
Tomorrow
Willow
Boat
Cake
Flesh
Coconut
Stone

Nobody
Bridge
Ice
Kiss
Bicycle
Adventure
Galaxy
Towel
Macaroni

Set the timer for a minute on each prompt. Aim to write for at least five minutes in total. Don't give yourself a breather – just keep going, getting everything, as much as you can, down. See where you go . . . I mean, this really could go on for all eternity.

You could work backwards, starting with a minute, then going down to thirty seconds on each, then seeing what association words you could come up with in twenty seconds, fifteen or even ten!

I spy with beautiful eyes

This works exactly like the game I spy, just a much lonelier version. LOL.

With your pen in your hand, in your room, on transport, wherever, give yourself a moment to find something or someone to focus on and once again, timed for a minute or two, write down everything you can about this one thing. It's like sketching but with words.

Next, try writing descriptions without saying what it is . . . How does this change your writing? This could make for some lovely poetry, forcing us to work a little harder.

Three

FINDING YOUR VOICE

'Be yourself.
Everyone else is already taken.'
OSCAR WILDE (possibly)

My general rule is to write how you speak. Quite literally – write how you talk. Don't write like a 'writer'. Write like YOU!

You are interesting. You are the only you that exists. So be yourself across the board, in all your ways. Make your words yours.

It takes A LOT to write. And even more to stick at a project without losing steam, burning the torch brightly until the end. It takes even MORE to share it. I get it. You are fully exposed. Your voice, your style, your ideas, your story – you might as well run naked down the high street. But now that we're all warmed up and toasty, I want to say well done. I know how much patience, determination, sacrifice, focus and energy it takes to keep at it. You should be so proud of yourself.

Now it's time to turn inwards. Without wanting to sound like a twit, we are our greatest inspirations; we are a living thing experiencing human life – so how do we express that?

At times writing can feel like staring at yourself in the mirror . . . probably crying. You are forced to look back at your reflection, to acknowledge who you were and accept who you've become, who you are becoming. IT'S A LOT. We don't always know how we feel or what we feel, let alone be able to find the words for these feelings. We might not know WHO we even are or WHY the hell we're even here.

But we can try.

I know. You might be worried what will happen if you look inside and express yourself. You might melt into a puddle, or completely fall apart like a house of sticks or be blown away by the wind. It's worrying what others might think – that you'll get judged, that you'll look stupid. But here is the place to try it out. This – your writing – is your wrecking room, your laboratory. Your playground and multicoloured ball pit. You are safe here. Have fun and see what you find . . .

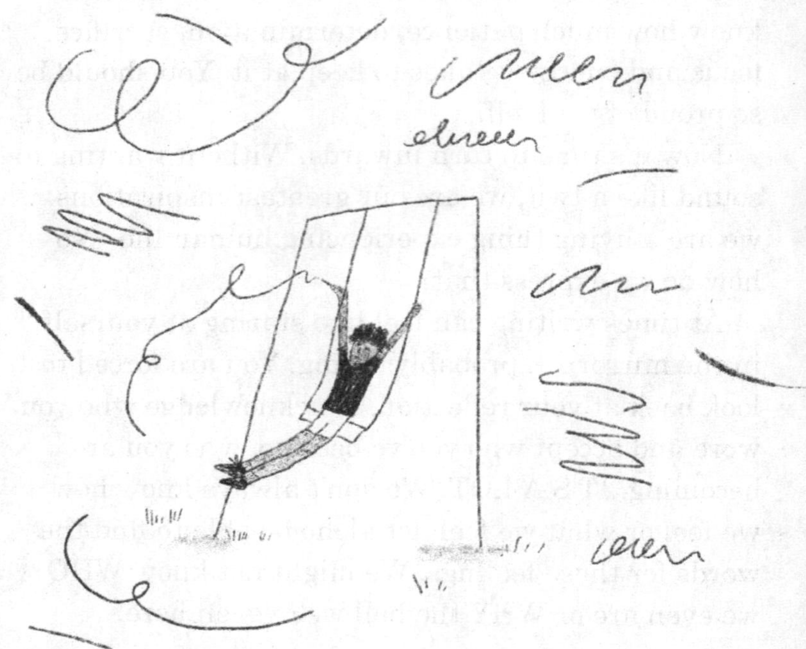

In finding your writing voice, who knows what else you might find? You might even find you. Your true self. This is where writing outlives the story; this is when writing outlives the writer. How can you lift your voice off the page and integrate it into your everyday life? How can we tune into that voice and find that inside confidence to hand the pen to our hearts?

Be true

My entry into the publishing world was ad hoc, accidental and massively lucky.

My current career in the publishing world is still all those things. I feel like I wing it and blag it every day. Like I'm always waiting for somebody to 'catch me out', but when it comes to the writing, the work, there is nothing fake about it. Because this is what I've always done. There's nothing to smoke out here; it's genuine, it's original and it's mine. (Whether somebody likes it or not is a totally different matter – and actually not my business!)

So don't cheat yourself – you can't trick your own brain into believing that you are 'the best writer in the world', and you don't need to – but you can write the best YOU can. Choose words that are true to you – the more unique to yourself the better. Don't worry if anybody else will 'get it' right now.

Don't know what that word means? Look it up or don't use it at all.

Can't find a word you're looking for? Invent a new one! It worked for Shakespeare and Roald Dahl . . .

The world craves original voices and stories from the heart, so if you're worried that your writing doesn't 'sound' writerly – excellent! More reason to write, babes!

Here are some jumping-off points to dig a little deeper into exploring how you sound as a writer, to stretch your muscles, experiment and see what you can do when you let YOUR writing voice sit in the driver's seat.

Checking in

Our emotions are kaleidoscopic and full of shades. We are never exactly the same moment to moment, let alone as each other. A simple way to find how you sound is to listen to you.

You can check in with yourself by scribbling down lines, sentences, pops of words and sketches all day long. Try not to analyse them or overthink them too much.

The senses

The senses are a great, easy way to begin. They activate and locate emotion, so it's a way to break down and simplify big feelings and a useful shorthand to express yourself to a reader.

Here are some ideas . . .

Smell

Quick – think of a person you love – how do they smell?

How do you know something belongs to somebody by their smell?

What are you thinking of?

How do you think you smell?

Scent to awaken memory and emotion

Scent is the sense thought to be most linked to memory and emotion. And memory, I'd say, is one of the skills a writer needs the most. Not because they need to remember facts – places, locations, names, times – but they need to remember how something felt.

After my illness there were many smells that I would find triggering. Catching the smell of a certain washing powder could easily send me flying back to the thick of it again! I smelt my 'mum' in Covent Garden the other day and I found myself looking for her like a lost child!

When I was feeling unwell, a therapist told me that smelling uses the front part of the brain that commands the rest of the body – I suppose so that if we were to smell a fire we could react fast. So when we are feeling anxious or distracted or can't quite grab on to our racing thoughts, if we smell something, it can help bring us back into the present. I've tried this before and it helped – garlic! My editor, Jenny, says that lavender helps her.

Scent roulette

This is probably my favourite exercise of all time. I first tried it at university and I took so much from it. We had a whole afternoon for it, a session that lasted about three hours. Our tutor came in like she had a surprise with her. And she did. Three cardboard boxes, each with several numbered picnic cups inside. She positioned the cups on a table and we watched on nervously . . . What was this experiment?

Each cup was filled with a different substance. Our tutor had picked things with scents that were deliberately loaded with memory and nostalgia, evocative and familiar.

Some were not easily recognisable. But I remember: coffee . . . sun cream . . . Marmite. The heady chemical smack of nail varnish remover.

In our own time, in silence, we went around smelling and guessing the contents of each cup. We made notes, we wrote some more, we went back, we smelt again. We spent time with each scent more closely, and wrote what came to us.

I remember a couple of my classmates crying in that session – that's how powerful this exercise can be if done well and if the environment is right. And how many more ideas this exercise can spark.

I have taken this exercise with me; it works really well in poetry workshops. I take twenty jars all filled with scent. I've added some new ones, including cigarette ash, perfume, bleach, chocolate, cumin, rosemary, star anise, burnt toast, WD-40, earth – earth is particularly amazing, as the smell doesn't immediately translate because it's mild and understated but it still invites so many memories and ignites some incredible poetry!

This exercise can easily be recreated at home. You could line up some scents to smell in cups or dishes. Perhaps you could ask a friend or family member to do it for you to make it more fun . . . and you could even wear a blindfold to make your senses work even harder!

Touch

The same exercise can be done with touch. You could line up some objects, fill tubs with textures and write about them. Here are some ideas:

- Feathers
- Bubble wrap
- A stone
- Water
- Custard
- A sponge
- Lentils, grains, rice, oats
- Crumbs
- Something bumpy, like a piece of fruit
- Something spiky, like a plant
- Something soft, like cotton wool or fabric
- Slime
- Sand

However, if this feels laborious and messy, why not just think about some of these and how they feel, and get some writing down using memory or your imagination?

The feeling of clay or dough/play dough

Squishing your hand into jelly

Water on your back in the shower

Your hand in ice-cold water

A warm bath

Taking your socks off in bed when your feet get too hot

The sun on your skin

Try writing the feeling of being tickled – that's hard, right?

Try to write the feeling of laughing. Of crying.

How does it feel to hurt yourself? To stub your toe or get a paper cut or bump your head.

Take a cup of hot water and a cup of water with ice. Feel the sensations, their differences. How do the temperatures make you feel?

Sound

The sound of silence . . .

What sounds can you hear if you really tune in? You might think you're in silence but are you actually? To me, even silence has a sound. It sounds grainy, muffled and painful. Sometimes scary. What does silence sound like to you?

Peace to me isn't found in silence. I like to hear the comforting sound of my neighbours rustling about. It makes me feel safe. On holiday I like to hear the breeze in the trees or sweeping across the ocean (or the clunk of cutlery to let me know it's time for lunch!)

I find background noise calming. Let's not forget that even as babies in the womb we would hear constant whooshing, pumping noises – that's why babies might need atmospheric noise to sleep.

If you really think about it, what can you hear NOW?

It's not particularly quiet where I work. I can hear the sound of my fingers tapping on the keyboard; cars roaring past on the road outside; leaves swishing in the wind; oh, the distant rumble of a neighbour's tumble dryer; a high-pitched voice from a TV somewhere; faint music from a car stereo; the bass of another car; the creaking of footsteps above; the buzz of the refrigerator.

What sounds can you identify?

You could think about other sounds. Cue them up, listen to them closely and then write about them. HOW do they sound? WHAT do they conjure up in your brain?

Here are just some ideas:

A spoon tinking in a cup

Snapping ribs of celery (which is apparently what audio artists in film and TV use to make the sound of bones breaking in horror films! YUCK! But also, great.)

Filling a jug with water

Blowing your nose

Footsteps

Humming

Thunder and lightning

A storm

The rainforest

Fireworks

Batter being whisked

Animal noises, like birdsong or whale song

What can you write down about the sounds? How do they make you feel? What do they remind you of?

Recording sound

When out and about, try recording atmospheres and environments, just on your phone, to capture energy. You could try a supermarket, a crowded place, a holy place, a school playground, a restaurant, the echoes of a swimming pool, snippets of conversation at a train station. How do the acoustics set up a world and let the reader know where they are?

When you get home, how can you translate those sounds into words? How can you show that same energy on the page?

The power of music

Never underestimate the sound of music! Hearing some songs can elastic-band me back to a certain place or period of time in my life and knock me off my feet. For about two years after my illness there were a few songs I couldn't even listen to.

Have you ever tried writing to music? It's an interesting exercise as it can change your pace and rhythm; it can encourage you to rhyme or push against patterns.

Here are some other ways you can use music to get you writing . . .

Put on a song you love and try to keep up with its pace, writing whatever comes into your mind. Can you write to the rhythm?

Get somebody you love to choose a song you've never heard and write to that. What are the lyrics about, do you think? How do they make you feel? You could look the lyrics up and see if you were right!

Have you ever wondered what the artist, writer and producer of a song were going through in their own lives when they created it? Does this alter your opinion of the music?

Give it context; What was going on globally at the time – politically, environmentally, socially? Did this have any influence on the sound?

You could write a new piece inspired by that song.

Find music, preferably instrumental, that is out of your comfort zone and write along to it. You could ask yourself . . . what does this song make me think about? If this song was scoring a film, what sort of scene would it accompany? Where was this song created?

Try writing fast to slow music.

Try writing slowly to fast music.

Write to a song that makes you reflective.

Write to a song that makes you feel GREAT.

BBC Radio 4 is the home to a magnificent show called *Desert Island Discs*. Each week a celebrity is 'cast away' to a desert island (not really, it's just a hypothetical scenario or else that would be a very different show!) and they can only take eight songs with them. The show is them playing each song and telling us why they chose them. The show ends up being very personal. Songs are such an ignition point for stories. They charge us, empower us, break us, connect us. The songs the castaways pick are not always necessarily their favourite songs, but they're songs that are pillars to their life – for good or bad, an 'X' on their personal maps that remind them of significant times in their lives. Could you do your own *Desert Island Discs* alone or with friends? Which songs would you choose and why? You could write about it . . .

Sight

An old brown wall.

Us humans see an old brown wall. It's old, it's been there for a while, it's a large brown wall, it is rectangular in shape, high and flat.

And that is that. An old brown wall.

If we look closer, though, we see that the wall is not flat at all; it is made up of many grainy bricks, each with their own individual marks, scratches, wear and tear, knocks and bruises. No two bricks are exactly the same. Plus, the texture of an old brick is always different. If we feel the wall, it might not be straight; it might be bumpy, curved even. It might have grooves. It might crumble. It's held together by cement, which also is not completely even. When we look closer again, we see the wall is not even actually brown – we find the colour red, the colour yellow, orange, pink, white, black, grey.

Can we find this acute amount of detail in everything we see? The leaves on the trees that change and merge, the petals on a flower, the way the sea meets the sky in a grey smudge? Your eyes are microscopes – practise looking closer into eyeballs, wood, skin, fruit, vegetables, the thread on a cushion, the wool of a jumper, the reflective rainbow in a bubble . . .

What do you see that you didn't see before?

Don't worry, not all writing has to express this level of detail, but it's great practice for our artistic eye and viewing the world differently.

Taste

As with the scent exercise you can do the same, but this time filling pots with tastes. Here are a few ideas:

Chocolate	Ginger
Chilli	Vanilla
Mustard	Garlic
Pickled onion	Cinnamon
Coriander	Toothpaste
Ketchup	Marmite

Writing about food

Food is probably my number-one thing to write about. It's so evocative and emotional.

I was running a creative writing masterclass once with a group of college students. It was a roasting-hot day in London and we were in an air-conditioned room close to Borough Market, a famous food market. I was co-hosting the session with another writer and I said to them that it seemed strange that we were in that room writing creatively when just across the road was a Mecca of inspiration.

Vendors serving stinky eye-smacking cheese, freshly baked empanadas, ribbons of transparent noodles, aromatic curries, bright red, thick tomato soup and sweaty griddled hot dogs. The tang of lemongrass, the energy of lime, burning turmeric, the song of melted chocolate, open pans of saffron and paprika paella spitting away happily in huge iron skillets big enough for a giant, the thick claggy sweetness of oily, buttery doughnuts frosted in the snow of sugar, the hit of Stilton, the rich earthy nuttiness of woody mushrooms and truffles like something from a pixie garden or the addictive smokiness pouring out of a jerk drum.

But more than that the smells all tangle into one another, the senses are forced to work hard, to investigate and explore. And the sights! The grassy shimmer of the Cinderella glass slipper of olive oil, brilliant pleased-with-themselves fresh juicy oranges clashing with vine tomatoes and dip-dyed radishes next to the clanging glamour of neon lemons. Snooty wine tasters and their purple bobbly noses, the iridescent moon glow of a shucked oyster shell, the twinkly bubbles inside a champagne flute, the polished leg of a baguette, the twisted neck of a green bird hanging upside down, the paper-thin stained window of Iberico pork and then the fearful lobsters floating in their tank, gently bouncing off one another like rowing boats, clambering over each other, claws clamped in elastic bands, eyes suspiciously twitching. And so many people to watch. On dates, as tourists, on lunch breaks . . .

We had a far better session once we got outside and went round the market, talking about our experience of food, tasting squares of cheese, wedges of fluffy bread, scoops of jam and chutney. What we liked, what we didn't. Some incredible and memorable writing came that day because we were driven by our hearts! By our bellies!

Food, for me, is storytelling. It is an understanding. It is a sense of a person, the language of love. It says a lot about a person. Where they are. Who they are. What is precious.

Try these ideas with food and write about the experience:

Put a square of chocolate on your tongue. Let it slowly melt.

Put a pinch of salt on your tongue.

Bite into a wedge of lemon.

Could you eat a jalapeño? A vinegary gherkin? A hot chilli?

Here are some questions you could ask yourself to evoke emotions, ignite memory and prompt fresh writing. You could even time yourself as with the free writing exercises. Focus on detail. Try using lovely descriptive words – with all your senses activated and each answer dressed in as much memory as you can. Where were you? Who were you with? Really encourage your words to work hard to paint the scene.

What is your earliest memory of food?

What is your favourite food?

Write about something you cooked for somebody.

What is the strangest thing you've ever tasted?

What food reminds you of home?

What food reminds you of school/education?

What are your comfort foods?

What can you cook?

What negative experiences have you had with food? (A time you were ill? Do you have any allergies?)

What food reminds you of tradition/celebration/ritual?

What food reminds you of travel?

What food did you used to hate but now love?

What are your greatest food experiences?

What is your relationship with food?

How has food shaped you?

How has food played a part in your life?

Choose one and expand on it, planting us in the moment. Have fun with switching characters and playing with perspective.

Hidden senses

Writing about my illness was a challenge, because my illness wasn't a thing. I couldn't see it, I couldn't hear it, I couldn't show anybody – but, oh boy, trust me, it was there. It was very real and very powerful. My family and professionals relied on me trying my best to describe what I was feeling and experiencing – which is what saved my life!

You can't see it, smell it, hear it, feel it, taste it, but at the same time . . . you absolutely can. It has a quality.

So let's not forget those intangible moments that are so sensory they are almost indescribable. This is the real sweet spot, how can we use words to scratch an itch? This is a chance to be super creative, to draw upon all of our personal references and be playful and original.

Can you try putting some feelings or experiences into words, bottling this stuff so that it IS tangible, so that you can translate it? Well, that's the real secret. Anybody can tell us the sky is blue, the grass is green . . . but how does heartbreak feel? What does embarrassment feel like?

I appreciate this is a challenge, but feel free to throw your poetic licence about the place, the rules out of the window and think outside the box. There is no right or wrong to ANY of this. Here are some ideas. If it's not too upsetting, maybe you could think about a time in your life you might have experienced:

Joy
Relief
Shame
Loneliness
Pride
Excitement
Doubt
Love
A kiss
Regret
Anger
Envy
Tension
Worry
Anxiety

OK. Well done. Here are some even harder ones . . .

Déjà vu
The space between being awake and dreaming
A hunch
Spirituality
That feeling when you 'just know'
Dread
Superstition
Attraction
Butterflies
Bliss
Dreaming
Connection
Or even more challenging . . .
How does love taste?
How does fear smell?
What does happiness look like?
What does the dark sound like?
What do you feel now?

Four

GATHERING IDEAS

Ideas are everywhere.

You might want to write about something that is completely separate from you. So where can you look for inspiration?

Ideas are everywhere. EVERYWHERE. All around us. The world is a rich, bottomless, melting-pot source of goodness. See your local area as a living environment, where every stone is a golden brick of inspiration, there for the taking. Out in the world, thoughts sprout; ideas are acorns ready to grow, and plots can blossom and bloom, twisting like ivy and vine round a locked gate, the pavement before you scattered with the mushrooms of beginnings.

Let characters walk past you as ripe as a peach to be plucked from a tree. Our ears can absorb real-life conversation like bees moving from flower to flower collecting pollen. Squeeze the juice from the fruit of everything. Every corner you turn is adventure, chance, opportunity.

No walk is ever exactly the same.

I'm asking you to drift. To take your time but switch ON. Tune in. Reach out. Stuff your pockets (with ideas – don't shoplift). Feast your eyes. Don't return home empty-handed (again, please don't shoplift). Every window is a microcosm, a glittering portal into a new world. A crumbling slice from the moist cake of life begging to be eaten.

There are buildings, roads, well-trodden paths, roots of trees, networks of nature running beneath our feet. Be connected to the universe, plug into the unknown, marinade in the sweet nectar of it all – put your head in the clouds, touch the stars, use your senses and collect. You are not only a writer now but an artist, a forager, a spy, a detective, a scientist, a hoarder, a qualified sniffer dog . . . Be really curious, be interested, be vigilant and aware and, above all, always, always, always be gorgeously, brutally, unapologetically nosy . . .

Magic-dust writer tips

Writing is not just found in the act of writing itself. It's about becoming the bacteria of life, growing in the gaps between . . . well . . . everything! Here are some simple tricks you can do when long writing stints aren't available to you for whatever reason – ways you can keep soaking up the wonder of the world and feed your creative mind while getting on with what you do best: living.

Keep everything

Keep everything. In a drawer, a shoebox, a file, an email account. If you've written on the back on an envelope, keep it, take a photo of it. Email it to yourself. Keep all the bits you write on, no matter how scrappy. You never know when the smallest word or sentence could end up being just the word or sentence you're looking for in the future.

Become a magpie

Pinch a little here and a little there. Be an honest thief of essence – of sense – of all the intangible nuances of life. Take ideas from the newspaper, social media, the radio, blend it with gossip overheard in the park, bits borrowed from TV, nick words you like in books, phrases your friends use in conversation. Dial into the frequency of real life (even if you're writing something set in fantasy). Ask questions when being told a story, interrogate, keep your eyes open, your ears peeled and your brain active and alert. There are stories EVERYWHERE happening all the time, ALL DAY LONG. Think of your brain like a piece of Velcro, or a net. Spread your wings, sharpen your beak, open your claws, constantly catching what you find. Collect, catch, collage and bring it back to your nest (your writing, obvs).

See living as research and the material around you as golden.

Ideas are like babies

Remember: ideas don't work around your schedule. They don't go to school or college. And they don't go to sleep when you want them to either. Ideas can cry out when it's least convenient, like a screaming baby, roaring wide awake on the bus, on holiday, in the shower, while you're trying to watch TV, fall asleep or even waking you up in the middle of the night. And if you ignore them? THEY JUST GET LOUDER! Let the ideas in – be ready, jot them down and don't forget. Once you write the idea down – even just a little note in your notebook or phone – it is usually satisfied and leaves you alone! Once the idea is caught you can dream on it, play with it and work on it when it suits you. Ideas can also be like ghosts. Ghosts that haunt you until you listen! So if you want a peaceful-ish life, it's worth your while to listen in and give the ideas somewhere to live in the pages of your notebook!

Technology

I am old school. OLLLLLLLDDDD SCCCCHHHOOOL. Without the K. I like traditional pen and paper. Bookshops. Writing, posting and receiving letters, rummaging around dusty old damp-smelling, rot-eaten junk shops and talking to real, actual human beings. And not because I'm trying to live up to the expectation of being a romanticised author stereotype. It's because I am an old gran mixed with a toddler and nothing in between. I still struggle with trusting technology. But I'd be lying if I said that technology hasn't improved my writing process, saving me time, effort, energy.

I write and take notes on my phone almost every day. This is great because ideas, thoughts, phrases and inspiration come at me when I'm the middle of something or when I'm away from my desk – usually when I'm trying to have a day off! Whether I'm in the supermarket or the park, I might write down a couple of words that come to mind, so if I ever need that snippet I've got them banked up. I suppose note-taking is a bit like taking a photograph – capturing a moment.

Take photos too! Record sounds and videos!

If I write notes, I always email or text them to myself to keep them safe. I actually wrote this while walking out of Brixton station and sent it to myself. Practising what I preach. Ta-da.

The voice-recording app on my phone has been so useful, particularly with dialogue or writing poetry. It's great for hands-free writing, PLUS hearing your work aloud can give you an understanding of your writing 'voice' and tone; does the work sound enough like you? Remember: we're not ever looking for perfection, but combing through our work in a fresh new light might help us improve our writing. Listening to your work can show you where punctuation might naturally fall, spot repetitions, highlight points you wish to stress and is a reminder that less is more; you might hear where certain parts can even be cut. The mics are usually pretty good on most smartphones (but it doesn't have to sound crystal clear). You could even play your story back to yourself on headphones. Take your story for a walk to the park! It's good to keep in mind that published writers never have control over where a reader digests their work – can you place yourself in the reader's or listener's shoes? It's important to step away from our writing spaces for perspective and distance.

I email ALL my work to myself. And I don't switch off my device until I see it arrive in my inbox. Not only does this back up my work, it also protects my work, and can be used to copyright your material.

Good writing is everywhere

Even when you're not able to write yourself at a particular moment, you can help keep your writing muscles strong and activated by acknowledging and digesting good writing. Good writing isn't found in the written word alone. Tune into phrases you like in books, yes, but also in lyrics of songs, the things people say on cooking shows, in films, plays, magazines, comics, on the radio and, of course, people in real life. Humans say beautiful and hilarious things all the time – stuff even the greatest writer couldn't write. I find presenters say funny things on TV – especially live TV – that is stranger than fiction; a person in a coffee shop drops a line of accidental poetry; an advert on a billboard makes me stop and think. You will find that poetry is everywhere, tumbling from the mouths of children and parents and shopkeepers, and written on chalkboards outside cafes. So jot them down, remember them, use them in your work.

This isn't plagiarism; this is recycling.

Up your downtime

If life is doing that busy thing and writing just seems an impossible ask, I say: lean into that. Don't stress about it, don't fight it, don't make yourself feel bad or guilty or force it. Instead, up your downtime, and that means **CHILL THE HELL OUT**.

Take care of your brain by doing . . . nothing.

It might feel still.

Too still.

Uncomfortably silent and empty.

There will come a time in your life when there is nothing to do except write. That time might not be right now – go with it.

Existing is still living. And living is still writing.

Sometimes doing nothing is doing everything.

And a bit of quiet downtime is more important than how many words you get written that day.

Junk and trash and rubbish can be good for you too

I used to think, Oh, I can't watch that – it's trash daytime TV or some cheesy sitcom. I'd think to myself, A real writer wouldn't watch this. You wouldn't catch a literary great watching this.

But now I say, hold on, if I enjoy it, then I'm gonna watch/read/listen to it.

Secondly, if it's successful, it's probably successful for a reason, so it's clearly doing something right –

maybe I can learn from it? What is its secret? (PS its secret could quite simply be as wonderfully harmless as making people feel good, which is really bloody important.)

Often it is HARD to be alive. Real life can be stressful. So spend an hour on the sofa watching strangers who have never met get married while eating a tub of ice cream if it helps. And do it with the confidence that you're not going to give yourself a hard time for it.

Also for your magpie sponge brain to remember: there's SO much good character study available in reality TV. It's a great way to get an insight into different situations and observe humans! Learn how people move, talk, collide, clash, argue, make up and live.

If I watch TV and I want something that's going to inspire me, grip me, make me feel or make me switch off, it isn't always going to be a documentary about Vikings. Sometimes I just want to watch the simplicity of a beautiful wedding cake getting iced in slow-mo.

And who knows – maybe it will inspire me to write a story about a cake that will go on to be a masterpiece. (Just saying.)

Writing on the go

You might be thinking, OK, so now I have to study, keep up with TV, be a good friend and be relatively pleasant to my family, clean my bedroom, make my bed, eat at least five portions of fruit and veg EVERY DAY, drink gallons of water, make sure my skin gets some vitamin D, read a book, maintain a hobby of some kind, walk a dog maybe, squeeze in eight hours' sleep a night, call my nan and now you want me to find the time to write too? ARE YOU JOKING ME?

I get it.

Plus, life is life, boy. Sometimes it doesn't care about our plans. Things happen, things move, plans change, time slips away and WE'RE ALL SO TIRED. We all have responsibilities that physically and mentally drain us.

REMINDER: If doing this makes you feel anxious and stressed, don't do it.

But, I promise, even five minutes a day of writing on your phone or on a notepad by your bedside is enough to get a writing sweat on and get the blood pumping. If you do it and find the words begin to flow, it will become addictive. What sort of differences will you notice – in your writing and in how you view the world? In your relationship with yourself?

So here are some ways to integrate writing into

your everyday, to make it a part of you, to live and breathe it.

Walk

If you are able to, walk. WALK. WALK. WALK. I have actually seen this really cool desk that is like a hamster wheel where you can walk continuously while you tap away. I like the idea of this. A lot. I have also seen a desk strapped to a treadmill – this is my jam.

But this is about getting outside too – because who has room for a human-sized hamster wheel? And how do you drink tea in one of those things without spilling it everywhere?

Fresh air, noticing, looking, observing, listening, plugging yourself in to the world around you. Walking is unifying your mind with the pace of your heartbeat. To feel the wind on your face, the rain in your hair, the sun on your skin is to feel alive. Vitamin D is so important for our well-being and it's easy not to be outdoors nearly as much as we should be; I feel like I'm always cramped behind a desk with a spine like a stegosaurus. Your ideas might become stale and limited if you're buried inside the static sterile four walls in which you live and dream, so the best way to recharge your inspiration is to get outdoors – see birds, meet dogs, feed swans (they're actually quite rude so don't, but the intention is nice), catch eyes, steal smiles, do that thing with a stranger where you aren't sure who is going to walk on which side of the pavement and you end up doing that awkward annoying dance thing. You might hear music, you might help somebody with their shopping, you might pick up a scarf dropped on the floor, you might get pooed on by a bird or see the police telling somebody off . . . All this and more is waiting for you just beyond your doorstep. Plus, being outside reminds us we are part of something bigger, something universal – you only have to walk past a bus stop to know that everybody has stuff going on; it isn't just you – and that can make us feel comforted.

Get outdoors, you little spy, you, and take notes.

Be a tourist in your own town

I love my city, London. I love the landmarks, the views, the skyline, the River Thames and all the magnificent buildings everywhere. I love the energy, the chaos, the bright lights and fast pace. Sometimes, because I live here every day, I find I take it for granted and forget to stop and take the time to appreciate it and admire all the wealth it has to offer. London is such a source for writing – for new ideas but drawing up memory too.

If I ever feel like my inspiration fuel tank is

running a bit low, it really energises my creativity to get lost, to try to see my city with new eyes once again. It's a great thing to do alone with a pen and notebook or a camera, or with friends. I love reminding myself that I live inside such a vibrant community and culture, full of millions of people each with their own unique lived experiences, and that is a REAL privilege.

I always pride myself on knowing London like the back of my hand. But I don't, and it's impossible to because it's changing all the time and there are always new treasures to be found. For example, I recently found out about a very special place in London called Postman's Park – a public garden. In 1900 the park became a memorial to 'heroic self-sacrifice', a sanctuary for 'ordinary people' who had died while saving the lives of others and who might otherwise be forgotten. Their names and stories are written on tiles on the wall like a mural. A visit there is peaceful, moving and emotional. And I reckon everywhere, no matter where you live, has its hidden gems.

When was the last time you got lost (in a pleasant way) in your local area? When you last walked around like a stranger and took your time to notice all the details – the history, the art, the politics, the literature, the music? When was the last time you explored your environment properly and tried to see it with new eyes?

Grab a pen and see what happens . . .

Renew your passport

Your imagination is a passport in itself. Renew it by whisking yourself off. With your passport there is no place you cannot go: the pyramids, the rainforest, Disneyland, your grandma's kitchen table, space, the past, the future . . . And all for free!

And no awkward photo of yourself either.

Words and pictures

'I'm always thinking about stories and I often see them as pictures. So writing helps me to get my ideas OUT of my head and onto a piece of paper. Then I can begin to shape them into a book.'
LIZ PICHON

Perhaps you might think you aren't a 'words person'? That's fine, but would you say you are a visual person, a picture person? The two things go hand in hand. Art, illustration, photography, fashion, cinema (the list goes on) are all excellent and important forms of storytelling too.

I remember going on a school trip to an art gallery as a very young child and we were asked to sketch a piece in the gallery. I chose a classic painting of two women. Sketching the painting made me see the women differently, even as a child, drawing what was probably (definitely) a very poor sketch: I noticed the women's expressions, their body language and their relationship. Back in the classroom we were asked to write a story inspired by the painting, using our sketch as a reference point. I still remember the piece I wrote today. It was a little script about two sisters fighting over a music stand, wanting to play the lead part.

Can you see how we can use art and images to go on entirely new writing crusades? That we can take an original seed of an idea and plant a whole new tree? That writing can happen anywhere at any time, germinated from anything? That we are surrounded by images and, because of that, we are surrounded by stories. You could find images on postcards, in catalogues, illustrations in children's books, on the front of greetings cards . . .

Writing to art is something I've always loved doing because it invites me to use a different part of my creativity. I find myself writing about shape and structure, colour and shade – it shakes up my vocabulary. How can what you see around you inform your writing? What happens if you let your eyes do the talking – does that influence the way you write?

Architecture

Another thing I think London is gifted with is its blend of historical and contemporary. You only have to stroll along the Southbank to see that. Take Shakespeare's Globe, for example: a 'reconstructed' Elizabethan playhouse set on cobbled streets. Its next-door neighbour? A giant boxy factory-like art gallery called the Tate Modern. Our landscape and environment can make excellent backdrops for our stories. You don't have to look far to build a new world.

> Go out and look at the buildings around you and see what they inspire. How can you include these buildings into your work? Drop them in new locations? Make new maps?

The jar

This was something I started doing during the 2020 Covid lockdowns when the days were long, endless and cast in a cold shadow of fear. It was an activity I did with my young son and it was a great way of being outdoors, getting fresh air and feeling connected and practical. Plus, it was spending time with my little boy and being creative and curious all at once!

We'd take our jars to the park and whatever we found that we liked the look of, or which was beautifully, hideously ugly or interesting, we'd collect in our jar. (I used washed-out jam jars but the jar doesn't have to be a jar. It can be a pocket or a bag.) We began with flowers, leaves, conkers, bark, grass, earth, sticks and stones, but once we got more confident we'd take home feathers, burst balloons on a string, a shoelace . . . We found a crushed brooch, a key, an earring, a dead wasp, bottle caps, coins and lots of broken china (some even from the same plate found in different places at different times), an ID card, a party popper and a shopping list.

When we got home we'd go through the objects we had found and lie them out on clear white paper. They'd always look really special laid out in this way, like pieces in an art exhibition. My son and I would talk about the objects, draw them, press them into play dough or glitter them and I'd write about them – just as little exercises, focusing on detail: colour, texture, shape. You can expand on the items, making up stories. Where did they come from? How did they get there? Who might have dropped them? Playing with new characters, past, present, future. Who might have found them if not you? You could use this exercise to imagine what somebody else could find – a map? Something of great importance?

Here is something I wrote about a party popper that I found lying in the grass under a tree:

Hold a grenade of joy.
Aim for the stars.
This harmless cheap thrill
when the night was ours.
This break-in-case-of-emergency rainbow
was the crackling smell of adventure.
The party might have died
but we will live for ever . . .

You could try writing about what you've found without saying what it is. You could write poems about what you've found. This could be the beginning of a whole story; this object could be the centre of a whole new world . . .

Supermarket

I love food shopping. And I love seeing what items people put in their basket. What does somebody's shopping list say about them? Even while queuing you could create a new character just by looking at the items in their trolley. Try not to stereotype but be original.

Try writing on some of the following topics . . .

What do you put in your basket and why?

Do you ever think about where that item comes from?

Could you describe the item without saying what it is?

What does it remind you of?

How do supermarkets make you feel? (They make me feel happy, safe and calm.)

What new thing could you pick up today?

What can you overhear in the supermarket?

Transport

Transport is a great source of inspiration. That's why sitting next to a stranger on a plane is such a 'thing' in movies; it's a total roll of the dice to be locked in with a new character, sometimes for HOURS on end. What might be an anticipated holiday for one could easily be a trip of dread for another!

Could you create two completely different characters and sit them side by side together and write a scene about their small talk? Maybe one wants to make friends and the other can't think of anything worse?

When you're on public transport, you could write about where you imagine all the passengers are going or coming from. You could imagine you're going somewhere else.

What journeys of significance can you think of from your past that stand out to you?

If you could be anywhere in the world now, where would you be?

Travel magazines are great places to find images of places you haven't been.

People watching

I love nothing more than sitting in the window of a cafe, with a massive wedge of carrot cake and a pot of tea, watching the world go by. And that means watching people. I LOVE people watching.

Think about the amount of people we are surrounded by and how there are no two people who are the same. How fascinating is that? Think about all our characteristics, charms, differences, quirks . . .

Think about characters you love in books, film, TV – why do you love them?

The next time you find yourself killing time, just watch. What do you see?

Sometimes the smaller the detail, the bigger the character.

Here are some questions I ask myself when people watching:

What is that person doing? Where are they going? Where have they been?

I might think about their clothes, their walk, their hair, their eyes, their age, their shoes.

I might wonder what is inside their pockets. Or bag.

I might wonder where they live and who with.

I might go deeper and ask myself what their relationship is like with their family, what their hopes are, how they were born, what they think the meaning of life might be. How their school years were . . .

Again, I try not to be presumptuous or judgemental. It's just curiosity, just jump-starting my brain.

The importance of being nosy and eavesdropping (and permission to do so)

I'll keep saying it: to be a writer you HAVE to be nosy. It's like being a spy but getting to wear bright clothes and not worrying about the hiding bit. To write we have to be NOSY AS HELL. From now on you are a classified eavesdropper, while of course remaining as polite as possible and retaining your subject's privacy. But to have a rich palette to paint humans from you need to know humans, with all their characteristics, nuances, eccentricities, quirks and, most importantly, flaws. If you want to be original you have to be truthful, so this means staying clear of tropes, clichés and stereotypes but tuning into reality. We want a catalogue of people up our sleeves at all times!

Here are some things to look and listen out for and maybe try writing:

How people eat

How people walk

The way people do their hair, and touch their hair when they're talking

The way people are dressed

The way people browse

How people interact

How people listen

What people do when they think no one is watching

What people do on public transport. (Ever watched somebody do their make-up on the bus? It's fascinating!)

How people speak on the phone in public

How people make small talk

The unsaid

Body language is really important to think about, including in your writing, especially when writing something without illustrations or visuals. How do we use our bodies and expressions to show our moods without saying them? We might be able to tell if somebody is having a bad day by the way they carry themselves. We can tell if someone is late by their walk, if they are excited, or if they are flirting. These might be a bit obvious – so what else can we see? Look about you and notice what is unsaid and how you can put this extra level of communication and language into your work. Tuning in to body language won't just help your writing but your connection with other people too! For example, you can tell if someone is being guarded or defensive just by how they hold their arms.

Here are some ideas . . .

How could you write about somebody who is upset without saying they are upset? How does their body language change and shift, such as their expression, their walk?

Could you do the same for someone scared or worried or excited?

Could you write how a person says something, describing whether their face shows if they mean what they say?

What about you? How do you react when you're tired, stressed, excited, nervous, happy, relaxed?

Other people's houses

Without being judgemental, of course, can you think of somebody else's house that you've visited?

We all have our own ways of doing things . . .

I used to go to this girl's house for sleepovers sometimes and the family ate their breakfast out of lunchboxes. It was just something they did.

Try thinking of a house belonging to somebody else from your memory. Close your eyes (after you've read the questions!) and really meditate on the environment. Try thinking about it practically first, i.e., geographically and physically, before moving in emotionally . . .

Where in the world is this house?

What is the area surrounding it like?

How does it look?

How does it feel when you step inside?

How does is it smell? (All houses have a smell!)

What is the floor like?

Is it a shoes-off house?

Are there pictures on the walls, ornaments?

Describe the furniture and the layout. If it helps, you could draw the house in your head or as a sketch . . .

What rituals or ways of doing things are different to what you're used to?

Do you feel like you 'fit in'?

How do the people who live there behave in the

space, respond to the space, treat the space, interact with the space? How does it make YOU feel?

What's in the fridge?

What's in the bathroom?

Where did you hang your coat?

Were you happy to return home?

Did you feel comfortable or 'on edge'? Did you feel strange? Or welcomed? Maybe you felt completely at home.

Write what comes instinctively and immediately. This may bring up lots of memories – go with whatever you feel comfortable with and let it all flood out . . .

Shoes

Shoes are another evocative way of getting new ideas and building characters. Have you noticed people's shoes? The shoes they wear and why they wear them? What do our shoes say about us and others?

Cracking the nut

Are you writing? If so, THIS IS GREAT! Well done! You might be tearing through the pages, filling up notebooks with a writer's bump on your finger as big as a mountain, but you might be thinking, what am I actually saying here? Or, what do I want to say? Remember: you have an opportunity to get a message across, to send vibrations and translate emotions. How do you want your reader to feel?

We don't just want an outer shell or a husk. We want that sweet juicy reward of a yummy nut.

How do we get to the point?

How do we do it cleverly?

How do we make sure our work has purpose and meaning?

Here are some crafty ways of getting your ideas across to a reader without force-feeding or ramming thoughts down their throats, but instead allowing them to think, respond and react for themselves. This is especially important when you're writing about activism, for example. It's possible to learn a lot from a good story if it's told well. Storytelling should be an experience – pleasurable, moving, inspiring, uplifting . . . whatever it is! Good writing asks questions, can interrogate, investigate, even make us want to make a difference! Stand back and let the reader take a look; allow the reader to do their bit in the exchange of storytelling.

Vegetables in the mashed potato

Did your parents ever hide broccoli in your mashed potatoes to try to make you eat it as a kid? (My parents didn't need to attempt any tactics like that with me as I had no trouble whatsoever eating absolutely everything on my plate at all times!) But maybe you know what I mean.

It's a sneaky way of saying we know you won't eat this healthy, highly vitamined stalk of green vegetable but you WILL eat this buttery, creamy, salty carby dream, so what I'm going to do, dear child, is blitz the broccoli INTO the mash and HIDE it, so you're taking in the healthy stuff without even realising.

It never works because potato is white and broccoli is GREEN, GUYS, and we're NOT STUPID, but I like the idea.

I like to think the same applies to writing. How can I create a world, a character and a story that is fun and adventurous while also slipping in the goodness?

I AM NOT SAYING THAT EVERY STORY HAS TO HAVE A 'MORAL' OR LESSON (because it doesn't). But in what ways can we serve our reader a bowl of creamy salty mashed potato while making sure they are taking in the healthy goodness too?

What do you want to say?

How can you say it without being too literal or heavy handed?

For example, my memoir was at times set up to feel like a love story. Or a thriller. I tried to lean into those traditional storytelling frameworks (the mashed potato) to secretly shout CAN WE PLEASE TALK ABOUT MATERNAL MENTAL HEALTH NOW?! (the broccoli).

Once a reader is hooked and invested you can take them anywhere. What do you want to talk about?

Trojan Horse

Do you know the story of the Trojan Horse? During the Trojan war an army of men try to take down a city they cannot enter. There is no way in. Then one of the soldiers has an idea . . .

The next day a massive wooden horse arrives at the castle gates – it is set up as a gift. And the horse is welcomed and taken inside.

Once inside the city, the horse opens up. It was hollow all along and inside is an army of men that basically jump out and cause hell and chaos.

OK, maybe we don't want to cause hell and chaos, but how can you bury what you want to say inside your story? How can you disguise what you want to say as something else?

A fantastic example of this is made by the comedian and activist Hannah Gadsby in her one-woman live show, the critically acclaimed *Nanette*. Audience members fill an auditorium, invest a good half of the show laughing their heads off at Gadsby's charming and witty jokes. Then, once they feel safe and warm and are putty in her palm, from out of nowhere Gadsby throws an alarming gut-punching attack of shocking truth at her crowd, following through with her activism, her point. Courageously changing gears on the show, the theatre falls silent; you could hear a pin drop. The comedy is the horse. And she is heard.

In one of my books for children, *Butterfly Brain*, I use rhyme as a way to hook a reader into thinking they are reading a modern take on a traditional cautionary tale, when really I was writing about grief and mental health. The rhyme helps to relax the reader, making them think they know what's coming next. The book combines the rhyme with bright and colourful illustrations so the read feels gentle and fun and age-appropriate too.

Sugar the pill

I'm not suggesting we go around pointing and laughing at our own and or others' misfortune – that just sounds horrible – but if you can get to a place where you can see the funny side of something difficult you have been through, I promise those hard edges begin to soften. It was the fictional childminder (and, OK, fine, philosopher) Mary Poppins who sang that 'a spoonful of sugar helps the medicine go down'. And she was right. Humour has been such medicine for me. Humour is your friend and if you are able to sugar the pill, it makes it a whole lot easier to swallow that chalky bitter medicine down. Who knows what wisdom is inside? Laughing at myself, at the past (with perspective and distance) has helped me process so much.

Even just smiling physically releases tension. It is impossible to feel true anger or fear when you are genuinely belly laughing (and, oh, I've laughed). I've also found that finding the 'silver lining' through humour allows others to ask questions and to open dialogue and conversation. Humour allows me to feel like an open book, ready to talk. It has also meant that others have felt relaxed enough to share their own experiences with me.

I get it – being able to laugh about something difficult is a whole new radical point to get to. And everybody is different; you just might not see the funny side whatsoever. I'm not saying you have to turn your difficulties into a comedy. I'm not saying you have to parcel up your memoir in a glitter bomb (but you could! I've seen work like this before and it can be hilarious and even MORE moving and powerful because it uses humour). But, at the same time, humour can be a defence tool, an avoidance strategy, a coping mechanism, a barrier and a reflex. It takes time to get the balance right. We all know that you can say what you like about a family member who's annoying you, but as soon as a friend jumps in, you're like, 'SHUT UP! HOW DARE

YOU?' The same applies to your story: you set the bar; you set the mood.

On the whole, here's what I've found:

If you're relaxed with your storytelling, listeners and readers will be relaxed too.

You're in the driver's seat. It's up to you to set the tone.

You're far more likely to keep readers entertained if you straddle both the light and shade.

Sometimes the dark stuff (scary, serious, angry, sad bits) actually hit harder when there is humour to cut through them, making them more impactful.

Give your reader a break to process and absorb the harder parts. Horror films quite often cut away to a fresh new morning so you can relax yourself for a minute to break up the heaviness.

Humour opens readers up. It's a great way to lure readers to your pages, and you will find yourself taken into their hearts.

Tell it like it is

But more often than not, there's no need for tricks and stunts – nothing does the job quite like telling YOUR STORY IN YOUR OWN WORDS.

No frills. No fluff.

Don't apologise for being yourself, for caring. That's your rebellion, your act of resistance, your punk.

And don't let anyone stop you.

A challenge

The next time you feel incensed by something – livid, powerless, raging, ignored, frustrated, out of control and feel like shouting at someone or sending an angry message – instead, like taming a wild horse, can you try to harness that fury, passion and energy? Can you channel your feelings in the right direction by writing about them? Don't censor yourself. Remove the pressure of making the writing 'good'. Get it all down. Use those feelings to create something positive. THIS is where that emotion belongs. What makes you mad? What p*$$e$ you off? If you cry, if your heart races, if you shake, if your writing is so messy in this moment it is barely readable you're probably doing it right!

The true power of words

Now go ahead and find the fire in your belly. Good rage can fuel revolutions, can warm us from the inside out. Inner charge can change, can grow, can connect. Good writing has the ability to build towers, knock down walls, smash glass ceilings and create bridges and even MOVE the world. And you can never be too young to find the inspiration, motivation and tenacity to start – take a look at Malala Yousafzai. Greta Thunberg. Anne Frank.

'I write because I believe with all my heart that stories matter – the stories we tell become our culture, our history, and so we have the power to form our futures too. Having a stake in that feels important.' – KIRAN MILLWOOD HARGRAVE

Thinking about the techniques we've discussed – the vegetables hidden in the mashed potatoes, the Trojan Horse, sugaring the pill – remembering that not all writing has to work hard, has to say something, BUT when it does, wow! Great words strung together in a brilliant order can be one of the most effective, influential, impactful and persuasive forms of expression available to us.

Think of Martin Luther King Jr's 'I have a dream'. That 1963 speech was so powerful it is still referred to today.

Songwriters such as Nina Simone, Bob Marley, John Lennon, Bob Dylan and Joni Mitchell have all used their platforms and skill for peaceful protest, spreading their anti-war, civil rights and social justice messages.

Riz Ahmed, Janelle Monáe, Childish Gambino, Young Fathers, Beyoncé, Jay-Z, Kendrick Lamar, Billie Holiday and Lauryn Hill have all used their talent, lived experience and platforms to speak about race.

How clever is that? To hide such meaningful messages in music that people can dance to?

You are young. You might be feeling a LOT. You have a lot to say. And a hell of a lot to write. I know it's scary to write about our personal views and opinions. It's daunting to roll up your sleeves and get political when we want a nice easy life. We might fret that we will get laughed at, shut down, debated, judged, humiliated; we might be worried we will offend somebody, say the wrong thing or not use the correct terminology. That it's 'not our place'. I know I feel anxious that if I say the wrong thing it will haunt me for ever. So sometimes it might feel easier to tread gently and say nothing. You might want to try to speak or write to make a difference but you're afraid of messing up or getting 'cancelled' so you stay silent . . . Well, how is that going to make an impact and leave a lasting effect? Then we feel worse because we stayed silent. I always say if the right intention is there – the heart, the grit, the feeling, the LOVE – that's what matters.

In these times, with the injection of social media, words can be heard, translated and transported globally within moments of them echoing from the speaker's tongue. But some words last much longer than fleeting social media memes. And need to be said.

I encourage you to speak out about what matters to you and the injustice you see around you. Use your voice to speak up for your friends and community. And if you don't know the 'correct' words just yet – come and stand, be there, hold hands, always with kindness.

It is completely possible to make activism artistic. You could write about the LGBTQIA+ community, climate change, disability rights, sexism, racism, consent, mental health, bullying, freedom, animal welfare . . . And there are so many ways to get your views across – through song, poetry, speech, theatre, manifesto, film and podcast. Have a play. It doesn't have to be explicitly direct. It doesn't have to be angry. You can make it peaceful and beautiful.

So long as you don't upset yourself in an unhelpful negative way, maybe you can use this safe space, here with this book, to help you think about what you stand for.

And it's more than OK not to know too.

'I write because when I was growing up, I couldn't find stories about people who look like me, with Muslim names, and brown skin, who grew up in England. I also write to work out my feelings, to connect with other people. Mainly I write because I love stories, and I love the characters who live in my head.'
SAIMA MIR

Take care

Writing about rights can be liberating and cathartic. It can connect us and empower us. But it can also be traumatic, painful and exposing too, especially if we write about our own lived experiences. It can reopen wounds and make us feel vulnerable and anxious. If you feel an urge to tell your truth, always make sure you feel supported and safe. Take breaks. Check in with yourself. You should never feel pressurised to talk about anything or share anything, especially if you feel uncomfortable in a bad way.

If you are standing with and supporting others, make sure you are sensitive and respectful. Listen. Research. And read the room.

And, above all, always, always, come with love.

Five

PLAYING ABOUT

'I write because I get lost in my head with ideas, character, worlds and stories, and if I don't get them out and onto paper my mind would be too busy. I write because it makes me SO happy!! I also write because I wanna make other people smile.'

NATHAN BYRON

This is my idea of fun.

The blank page is not a threat but a chance. Here are some fun sparks and scratches, places to begin. The good news is, you never have to go far to find inspiration, especially if you are writing about yourself. Inspiration and ideas are right under your nose. Here are some easy, cheap, fun ways to get started.

We don't always have to write about ourselves. We can have fun making up new worlds, creating new characters and story scenarios. Writing 'make-believe' isn't pointless – using our imaginations is an incredible way of learning more about ourselves. It's another way in . . . and of seeing what comes out.

Ways to play

And then . . .

A wise woman once said, if you don't know where to start, try the beginning. (Or something like that.) It's really difficult to know where a story actually starts, so I just want to remind you that any point along the way you can have fun editing, chopping up and rearranging the order of things. Sometimes it's easiest to write things out as they were, as they happened (in real life or your imagination) in chronological order.

Let your pen lead your head. With this exercise, land your pen on the page, or your fingers on the keyboard, and see where you or your character goes next. Enjoy the spontaneous element, the surprise . . . Go with it and remember there are no rights or wrongs. These are directions for you to write what happens next, and see where your thoughts take you.

You turn a corner . . .

You open a door . . .

You look out of the window . . .

Look up . . .

Look down . . .

You open a letter . . .

You answer the phone . . .

Choose a book, any book . . .

. . . from any shelf anywhere. Don't think about it too much.

OK, being totally honest, the first book I've gone for is . . . *The Count of Monte Cristo*, Volume 2. (I didn't even know there were two volumes. In fact, I didn't even know I owned this book. So I clearly haven't read this book.) It's a really nice edition, though: leather-bound with gold loopy writing. Perfect.

You could use this example or pick a book from your shelf at home or a library.

Can you think of a whole new original story/poem/script/comic that could own this title?

If you need more inspiration, open the book and choose words and phrases to inspire you. Try not to overthink it. Open a page, any page, drop your finger down and write down the words you find.

I've got: Piano. Conscience. Arm. Tottering. Murdered. Sleep. Gallop. Flash of light . . .

Can you see how already I'm using new language? I'm exploring with vocabulary, forcing myself to write out of my comfort zone. I've never used the word 'tottering' in any of my work before, but you know what? I kind of like it! You could have fun writing poems or scripts in this way.

You could choose more than one book and have the books talk to each other with words! Pretty out there, but why the hell not?

How to make your writing be felt

In the art of 'telling a story' the best way to *tell* is to *show*. (Simple, right?)

Chekhov said something like, 'Don't tell me the moon is shining; show me the glint of light on broken glass.' He's right. The 'light on the broken glass' is much more enchanting than stating that the moon is shining.

If we want to say, for example, 'Kamara took the train' we are asking our reader to do quite a lot of work. We all have different versions in our mind of a train (and indeed who Kamara could be) based on our own experience, knowledge, history, memory and imagination. If 'Kamara took the train' is the outline, it's up to us to fill in in the detail.

Let's make this exercise simpler and say we've already set up Kamara and we're moving the reader along. We want to plant them in the scene with Kamara. Or, even better, as though they are Kamara. We are giving them a chance to escape. To live somewhere else for a bit. Which train? What kind of train? Where from? Who else was on the train? How did it smell? Was it hot or cold? Was it clean? Was it packed or empty? Is this routine or unusual for Kamara? Did Kamara get a seat? And how was the light coming in? How was Kamara feeling? What was Kamara wearing? What noises were there in the background? Who was Kamara with? Where was Kamara going?

Try now, as an exercise, to write Kamara taking the train, being as elaborate as you possibly can . . . Imagine you are there and describe what it's like.

Beautiful! Do you see how showing sets the tone and places the reader in the scene?

However, it also doesn't have to be a lot. And it doesn't have to be poetry. See the tiny changes I've made to the sentence here, but notice the big impact they've had on the story . . .

'Kamara took the same train everyday but . . .'

But what?

'Kamara took the bag and boarded the train.'

Now I want to read more . . . What bag . . . ?

Again, this is about the art of 'telling a story', but there are other tricks you can use to help you do this, like telling the train scene in the first person, so we feel Kamara's feelings and thoughts – we ride the train too. This is where storytelling gets exciting. If we wanted to, we could have Kamara's mind elsewhere, mulling over a problem. The poetry would be that we see Kamara travelling physically but feeling internally stuck. Then we have conflict, irony, contrast – and that's when we can play with our readers.

No words

Silence can be the most powerful tool a writer can use. Sometimes there are just no words to describe a feeling. We can place silence in a piece of text. A pause can be a shock, a dramatic break or a chance to reflect. A moment for a reader to fill in the gaps. It can offer an opportunity for comic timing – comedy is all about timing and it's not always fast! Suspension can keep a reader glued to your work. Action can also come into play here – nothing was said but a door was slammed or a kiss or a gift was given . . .

Many people find silence uncomfortable and awkward, and find the need to talk through the silence to try to 'break it down', but sometimes this only shines a light on the silence!

Character

Sometimes we get so focused on what happens in a story that the authenticity, originality and sincerity becomes lost. Sometimes we think loads has to happen to keep a reader gripped and paying attention, that a plot needs to be firing in all directions, working on many levels and the stakes need to be super high. As a reader, **we come for the story but we stick around for the voice** – the friendship and connection we make with our characters. How I see it, anybody can write a plot – if you had to, you could get all your friends over for a pizza night and ask them all, what could happen in my story? and ideas would be flying at you. This is what happens in writing rooms and board meetings at offices. Story will come; it's who tells it and tells it well and how it's told that makes it stand out.

Remember: a character doesn't have to be 'nice' to be liked. A character doesn't even have to be 'liked' at all to be compelling (but it helps). How many times have you read or seen a character do horrible stuff and you still find yourself rooting for them? (I actually find these make the best lead characters.)

We want characters we see ourselves inside, who we can relate to, who we can empathise with. And that means bye-bye perfection. Just like in real life, just like the one you're living – and in the bonds we make with the people around us – we are not looking for 'perfection'. Our characters are just like us: human beings who make mistakes, who get things wrong. Who get sad and angry. In the books we love we are looking for characters who remind us of us. Really, the more of our DNA we get on the page the truer and ultimately more likeable our character will be.

You might be writing in the first person from your lived experience but to a reader you are still the narrator, the storyteller (more on that below). You don't have to be 'liked' and always be 'good'. You can still make mistakes and 'bad' descisions. You are a human doing your absolute best!

For me, the hook is the voice; that is what you are investing in. A lot of the voice will come from you. If you don't want to write 'your' thoughts down, you can conceal your own traits, ideas, characteristics, charms, in-jokes and opinions into your characters. You could remix your personality with a friend's, into the body of a celebrity, a stranger, a kid in school or even an animal. Here are some excercises that can help you create new characters, people who don't exist until you magic them up . . .

Miss Milk

My sister, her friend and I used to get the same train to school every day, and opposite our platform was a track with a train going the other direction. Every day we'd see the same woman standing in the same place with the same tired face. She was really small and slight and like something from the past. Honestly, I'd sometimes wonder if she was a ghost. She'd wear a long grey mac that went all the way down to her ankles and was buttoned up to her neck, with brown tights and flat little brown shoes. Her haircut was short and round like a choirboy's and the colour of really milky tea. She'd wear big bottle-top glasses. What she didn't know, but we did, because we'd be standing opposite her, was that graffitied in giant white letters on the face of the platform beneath her, where the tracks were (where she stood every day), was the word 'MILK'. We just couldn't believe the irony of that, and she soon became Miss Milk. We made up a whole life for Miss Milk. We would spend the whole twenty-minute train journey deciding her job, her home life, what she ate for lunch and did for fun. What she was like as a child and what she'd be like as an old lady.

Miss Milk never did make it into a book. Oh, wait a minute – I suppose she just has!

Can you think of a Miss Milk? Who do you see and wonder about in your daily life?

When writing new work – fictional work – think about flooding your world with characters. It isn't just your lead character who needs to be interesting.

EVERYBODY IS INTERESTING.
EVERYBODY IS INTERESTING.
And that includes you!

A bag of stuff

Charity shops are amazing, and perfect for coming up with new ideas and inspiration. Most of my clothes are second-hand. A lot of my books and furniture are from charity shops. I have bought a LOT of great stuff over the years, but there have been two items that I purchased solely as writing tools that stick out in my memory, which I'll share with you now, as they are constant sources of inspiration for me.

A bag of buttons

From a charity shop I bought, for fifty pence, a bag of buttons. The bag itself is lovely: a soft silk drawstring bag in lilac; inside the buttons are all different. They're completely random. Some are broken, some are old, some are new. Some are plastic, some are metal, some are wooden, some are wool. Some are silk, some are sequined. They are all different shapes and colours. They are all beautiful. This bag of buttons is small and light. I take it to workshops with me as it's perfect for a warm-up exercise.

Usually I lay the buttons out on the table and writers come up and choose a button that they are drawn to. We spend time writing and describing the button: literally, physically. We zoom in on the button, describing its features and character. Then we start building in reverse, beginning with the button: what item of clothing was the button attached to – a jacket, a dress, a school uniform, shoes? – until we have invented a full costume. We then create a whole new character from our imaginations. If we are looking to conjure up a 'character' that represents 'us' but is not 'us', allowing ourselves to write explicitly and deeply about our own experience, it is best to start from scratch in this way. We can spend time giving the character a personality, an identity and a voice. A simple technique to get started would be to ask your character their feelings towards this item of clothing – what is their relationship with it? – could you write them finding this item? Or write them putting the item of clothing on?

Sometimes I pretend the buttons are found – in what world, time, life would I find a button like this?

It could even be the start of an adventure . . .

Maybe the button collection is the story . . .

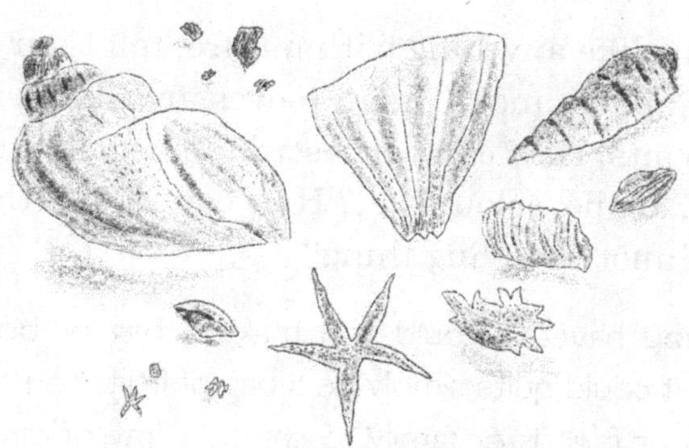

A box of shells

This is the second item I bagged from a charity shop, which gives me so much back. Shells are so beautiful and compelling to write about. Especially as a city girl, it's not often I stumble across a shell unless it's a mussel shell on the backstreet of Soho from some spilt bin bag outside a restaurant!

So, yet again, the shells can be laid out on a table. In sessions I invite writers to choose a shell that they are drawn to. The idea, of course, is to write about the shell, but this time to imagine where they are in the world, their relationship with the shell and why they chose the shell they did. Often this is a really nice way into writing about our relationships with nature, travel and ourselves. (Although during one of these sessions I did end up going on an unforgettable and unnecessary tangent by writing about my dad's toenails, so . . . keep open-minded!)

Shells, like anything with nature, tell their story in their appearance. Their grooves are like wrinkles, fingerprints. How can we describe the shell, its texture, shape, colours . . .? How can we tell the story of another living thing?

Do you have or could you make a bag or box of stuff? It could quite simply be a bag of fruit. You could ask your friends or family to create a tray of random objects for you and then choose one. Or you could lie them out and write about them all.

You can collect things for your bag of stuff from different places. It could even be things you find on the ground.

Photographs and postcards

I know writers who use photographs and postcards as inspiration for characters. I collect images to pull out during writing sessions, inviting writers to scribble down why they chose the piece they did and their initial reactions and reflections.

You could have somebody choose a card or photo for you. Locations can fuel inspiration for new landscapes; buildings can become the focus for an event – places that we might not have come up with on our own without a prompt. Images of animals or mythical creatures can spark new character ideas.

Or you could choose cards of abstract art to inspire backdrops to place your characters . . . Use colour, shape and texture, go with what comes to you and think outside the box. Photographs of strangers' faces invite us to impress personalities on to them, creating characters. You can switch and swap perspectives and viewpoints with the faces in the photographs. You could even interact faces in photos with other faces in photos. Create scenes.

Clothes

Get a friend or relative to pull together an outfit from their wardrobe and send you a photo of it. The outfit can coordinate or clash. Then set yourself the challenge of creating somebody to wear that outfit.

We should always try to avoid stereotypes – check in with yourself that your writing is original, unique and not lazy. Instead, flip the script, use your wonderful imagination. How can you write characters without getting caught up in expectation?

Who would wear an outfit like this?

What is their name? What are their interests? Their favourite things to do? What is their job? Where do they live? What is their favourite song? What is their greatest wish? Their deepest regret?

Where is your character going in this outfit?

What are they doing?

How does your character feel when they wear this outfit?

How do others respond to this outfit?

Could you, as a challenge, give the clothing a fantastical or magical element?

An object

Ask a friend or relative to pull out an object for you or send you a photograph of it.

Can you describe it?

Does it have a purpose?

Could you describe the object as though this is the first time you've seen anything like it?

How does the object look?

Feel?

Weigh?

What is it used for?

How do you feel about the object?

How could a piece of work be centred around this object? It could be involved in a robbery, a quest, an argument, a clue or a piece of evidence…

Have you ever written a ghost story?

Have you ever written a detective story?

What about an adventure story?

Now is your chance!

Do you know what I mean?

Think about how people talk and express themselves. For example, about a year ago I began to notice I had started saying 'Do you know what I mean?' all the time, even when it wasn't needed. 'Shall we have pasta for dinner, do you know what I mean?' I then noticed my partner had started using it, and it annoyed the hell out of me because I was already getting on MY own nerves. Now he was too. Then my sister started using it and I thought my head was gonna explode. Now all my friends use it for everything, out of context, and I no longer use it even though I started it in the first place! Keep an eye out for catchphrases like this – what turns of phrase do you and your friends use? Where did they come from? What do they mean? How have they grown and adapted?

One of the questions I get asked the most in workshops is how you go about not making all your characters/voices sound the same when you are writing more than one. This is hard, but I think these sorts of catchphrases are a good easy way to start. You can use them to make your characters sound realistic and three-dimensional. You could have a character who always says 'to be honest' when they are not even revealing anything of any particular value. Or a character who calls everybody 'love'. These slight details will really help lift your dialogue and make your characters sing like humans.

Elephant in the room

As an exercise, practise talking about a subject without saying the one thing you truly want to say. For example, let's say we've got a character who we know has recently lost their grandad. They might bump into a friend and talk about EVERYTHING they possibly can except for this. What does this say about that person? Try this when creating a character or write from your experience.

Plot

I am NOT the greatest of planners. Surprisingly, many authors don't plan their work before they start writing. Or at least not everything. Writer Rose Tremain advises 'don't plan the ending' and I have to agree. Sometimes, even as the writer, it's nice for me too to not know what happens next.

I love the act of writing. I love making characters so convincing that they show me what happens, where we are going, what we are doing. It's part of the fun, letting them steer the ship, and I'm like a vessel, a host, that they're using to tell their story. I suppose this is the 'mindfulness' part of writing that I so badly rely on – it's part of the escapism, the fun, the distraction, the magic.

Enjoy these moments of musicality and poetry. Hand yourself over and surrender to the pen. People play computer games for hours on end, people read, people make tiny pistachio macaroons for no reason or stitch quilts; people run, people play the piano or basketball or golf or meditate – we write. That is what we do. That is how we escape. That is our freedom. Our happy place.

Why would I want to go to a party if I knew what was going to happen at the party? And if writing is a party, let me have fun!

Seriously, I love nothing more than showering, only to get into clean pyjamas for a good old day at my computer of NOT KNOWING WHAT ON EARTH IS GOING TO HAPPEN, GUYS . . .

'I write because I get ideas, and I really want to find out what happens. I write because I find so many things funny or absurd, and it is delightful to share funny stories with readers. I write because I love to read, to hear stories, and to tell stories'
FRANCESCA SIMON

That said, you might be a planner. You might need Post-it notes all over your wall like you're hunting a serial killer. All your characters might need passports before they can even land on a page. I know writers who don't even think about writing creatively until they know every beat and what is going to happen for every scene. I mean, brilliant, but it scares me. It's daunting and makes writing sound like 'work'.

If you are writing from true lived experience, then you don't need to plot or plan.

Just write. You can flip the structure and experiment with timing afterwards, but focus on getting your story down first.

I tend not to 'teach' plot and structure because I find it, on the whole, quite . . . well . . . boring. I think it can make writing sound kind of manipulative and prescribed. It takes away the natural beauty of a piece and can limit you from being in touch with the world around you – both in reality and any world you've created in your imagination. But there are lots of formulas and plot templates available online and in books that I'm sure are very useful and helpful and probably the secret weapon into writing a hit.

My shorthand is this: **What does my character want? What does my character need?**

By the end, the character realises that what they want is not what they need.

But all the ideas are taken . . . aren't they?

YES. THEY. ARE. We live in a world where we've 'seen it all before'. Sometimes I read an idea back to myself and panic that I've stolen the plot of a film, smushed it with a book I read and then titled it to a song I heard on the radio five minutes ago.

All stories are based on fairy tales/Greek mythology/folklore and if it's not, Shakespeare definitely nabbed ALL the story scenarios for himself. And if HE didn't – trust me, *EastEnders* has. Believe it or not, there are only really a few possible storylines. For example, the 'rags to riches' storyline like poor old Cinderella, or 'the rebirth' (when somebody evolves over the story arc, ultimately becoming a 'better' person) like in *Beauty and the Beast* or *The Secret Garden*, or a tradgedy like *Hamilton*. There are always repeats and crossovers. Don't let that put you off – there is space for ALL stories in all their versions, and there is NO story out there that is exactly yours because **you are one of a kind**. It's not what the story is but how it's told that counts.

You might feel like you're stealing, but everybody is stealing a bit; it's impossible not to. (Please don't actually steal, though – it's called plagiarism and copyright infringement and it's very serious) – but borrowing and embroidering is fine!

So if we take away the pressure of coming up with that all-guns-blazing fireworks and theatrics, what we are left with is how we tell a story, and that's why nailing the voice is so important. That there is the gold.

Six

YOU ARE ENOUGH

It's time to dig a little deeper . . .

Remember when you picked up a pen for the very first time? Remember when you wrote and imagined just for writing and imagining's sake? When you weren't worried what anybody else would think? When you felt proud of your work, when you wanted to show and share it with somebody you loved?

Well, that is who we will be handing over the pen to now.

We're going to dig a little deeper . . .

Childhood bedrooms

If anything comes up here that you find uncomfortable or difficult, you don't have to go anywhere you don't want to. That said, feel free to mine down as far as you like or feel you can with the exercises and make them your own. These tasks are simply ignition points and prompts to spark intrigue, inspiration and curiosity. This is not a challenge or a test. There is no right or wrong. It is a chance for you to begin . . .

If you cannot think that far back or would prefer not to, that's absolutely fine – you can use your current or a recent bedroom. If the whole exercise is too uncomfortable for you, you can choose any room or invent one! (Home, travel and lifestyle magazines can be really useful for new locations! There's no need to buy them – see if you know someone who can pass on their magazines when they're finished.)

Picture your childhood bedroom. There is usually one that sticks out the most – go with that one.

Have a read of the questions below and then close your eyes and marinate in the answers, building the room in your mind as it comes. I imagine it like big broad strokes with a paintbrush, then filling in with more detail, but go with however it comes to your mind. Maybe you see it as boxes or from a bird's-eye view; maybe you see it in lines like an architect's drawing or as a sketch; maybe it's three-dimensional or like a film. Maybe it's totally abstract and surreal. Maybe today you can't get anything, and that's fine too – there is an exercise below to help you.

To begin . . .

Where in the world is the room?

Where in time is the room?

What is the shape of the room?

What are the walls like?

Is there a window?

What's the view? What can you see?

Is there a door?

What is the sense of space? Floor space, ceiling space?

What is the light like in the room?

What is the air like in the room?

Is there furniture?

Free writing

Write, uninterrupted, for five minutes on your childhood bedroom, being as detailed as you can. At this point we are thinking of physical attributes to set the scene: colours, furniture, layout, etc.

Now you could ask yourself some more questions, like:

Do you share this room?

How is it decorated?

How would we know it was yours?

What 'stuff' is inside it?

Decorate it in your mind, fill it with a sense of you – you might use possessions, ornaments, pictures . . .

Free drawing

DO NOT WORRY about your drawing skills! Nobody will ever have to see this. Set the timer again for five minutes.

Draw your bedroom, being as thorough as you can. Feel free to colour, list, code, scribble – there are no rules. Have fun with it! (Once a guy in a writing workshop tore up a whole pad of paper and made a three-dimensional room! You don't have to do this but feel free to be as creative/interpretative as you like. You can use collage, photos, clay . . .)

Speed exercise

Write on the following for one minute each, pausing in between to absorb the next question:

Does your childhood bedroom reflect you and your personality at this point?

What are your feelings towards your bedroom?

What does your bedroom know about you that nobody else does?

Is there a time your room has seen you angry?

Is there a time your room has seen you happy?

Do you have a particular memory from your room?

Did you room 'hold' you? Keep you safe?

Dear bedroom . . .

Earlier on I think I told a lie when I said scent roulette was my favourite exercise of all. I reckon this might be my favourite. Why? Because it's SO personal. It reveals so much about a writer and a person and it is incredible for waking up that inner writing voice. And it can take place anywhere at anytime without props or fussiness. It is unadulterated, pure, simple and bold. It gives you the possibility to have complete authorship while engaging your memory and experience. And there is plenty of room for humour and play, which allows us to unlock our inner voices! With this exercise, it seems impossible for writers to NOT write from the heart – it's completely unavoidable. Even when writers try not to write the truth it seems to pour out in the silence – it's what isn't said that says it all.

The task quite simply is to write a letter to your bedroom however you'd like, beginning with two words: 'Dear bedroom . . .'

And see what comes.

How do you feel about your current bedroom? Could you describe it? Put it into words.

How about your home?

New character bedrooms

JUST FOR FUN maybe you could try the same experiment but with a completely new character's bedroom? Don't overthink it – just write. The bedroom could be in the past, present or future. It could be set in reality or fantasy; it could be what seems like an 'ordinary' bedroom but with a twist or magical element – remember the wardrobe to Narnia? It could be hidden at the bottom of the ocean or on a mountain, in a tree, underground or with the stars. Let your imagination do the talking – **no response is too ridiculous**. You could also draw this new bedroom to see it as a sketch, to get a sense of it.

Think about whose room this is. A human, animal, monster, 'being'? What do they look like, where have they come from, where are they going, what do they want?

You could try writing in the first person. You could introduce your younger self to your new character – where or how would they meet? Why have they come together?

You could think about introducing an object, perhaps one from earlier, and play out what would happen.

You could re-introduce one of the earlier exercises? Meet as strangers on an aeroplane? You could set them on a wild quest together?

Play with twists and turns – what can they teach each other? What can they learn?

Identity

In a way, we are all writers. We all tell ourselves stories all day long. About other people, about the world and about ourselves. That's that because of that. They are like that because of this. Have you ever wondered who you actually are? Or are you living a narrative that others and yourself have created for you? A narrative like me not being a numbers person, so I avoid maths. For example, in basic terms, let's say one day you wear a red jacket. Before you know it you're the red-jacket kid and your favourite colour is red. Will you then begin to choose red things for yourself? Is red your favourite colour now? Do you even like red?

Another low-level example: once as a kid I told my mum my favourite fruit was mango. Before I knew it every birthday it was like I was a mango fanatic. My mum would buy me everything from mango body scrub and lip balm to a mango pencil case and mango pyjamas. Mango socks. Mango notebook. Even my grandparents got involved – a mug saying 'I HEART MANGO', a utensil specifically to peel mangos. Mum would buy me so many mangos to eat that I couldn't stand the sight of them! They festered and went rotten; I'd hide them to pretend I'd eaten them to keep her happy.

This is a narrative. A story. Mangos are delicious, yeah, but it's not, like, my thing. (Are you wondering if mango knickers exist? Oh, trust me, they do.)

Sometimes we say or do things to fit in. I know I do. It's instinctive and part of survival. Have a look at the below . . .

Who are you?

Take a minute. Soak up that massive question. Write what comes. Cover everything from music, colours, films, opinions, politics, values, viewpoints, interests.

Here are some more interesting jumping-off points to help you if you want more direction or get stuck:

If you were a character in a book, how would you describe yourself?

How do you feel about yourself?

How would other people describe you?

How do you feel you come across as a first impression?

What is your place in the world?

What do you believe in?

What do you stand for?

What makes you unique?

Try writing a poem. Try writing it as a manifesto. Try it as a speech. A song. A stand-up comedy show. A letter to a loved one.

The mirror

When was the last time you looked at your reflection? Really looked at it? I've done this exercise with teenagers and a bunch of hand mirrors many times and we all end up crying by the end.

Our faces are exposed to the outside world all day long but we rarely stop and look at our own. I personally find this exercise really challenging (mostly because my dad's face seems to emerge out of mine like some cartoon hallucination and I feel like I'm trapped in a horror film) so I can appreciate that this

might be difficult. We are also very quick to pull ourselves apart and highlight the bits about ourselves we don't like. Well, not today.

As an exercise, are you able to look at your reflection without being judgemental? Can you describe your face as if you were talking about something different without saying what it is? Here are some ideas:

As a piece of art.

As a stranger.

As a landscape.

As objectively as possible.

As matter-of-factly as possible.

As if seeing it for the first time.

Or start with yourself, inside out . . .

Interview with you

When was the last time you sat down and had a good conversation with yourself? Try these . . .

You could create some more of your own – why not practise them over a month or so and see if the answers change?

I remember . . .

Write the words 'I remember' and see what comes . . .

I wish . . .

Write the words 'I wish' and see what comes . . .

I'm great at . . .

Write the words 'I'm great at' and see what comes . . .

One day . . .

Write the words 'one day' and see what comes . . .

I've never . . .

Write the words 'I've never' and see what comes . . .

Tomorrow . . .

Write the word 'tomorrow' and see what comes . . .

School Days

From the first day of school, our days are filled with memorable teachers, friends, the uniform, school dinners, P.E., packed lunches, trips, concerts, plays, embarrassing moments, passing notes in lessons, bad coffee breath, getting told off, exams and sports day . . . For me, there is both humour AND trauma to be found when I look back over my time at school!

Unfortunately, school isn't a great experience for everyone. For some people it's a complete mixed bag of emotions; others describe their school days as 'the best years of their life'.

Can you write about your time at school? How is/was it for you? It can be in the style of memoir, a poem, a script, an article or an opening to a novel.

Here are some jumping-off points:
What did/does the building look like?
What was/is the playground or outside area like?
Describe your uniform, your shoes, your bag . . .

Write about a stand out teacher (for good or bad) . . .

Who did you hang out with?

What were/are your favourite subjects and why?

Can you recall a time you surprised yourself?

What were/are the school dinners like?

Can you list any significant memories? Funny, sad, painful, heartbreaking . . .

Have you ever had to visit the school nurse? What happened?

Did you take part in any performances? Celebrations? Out-of-school activities?

What about your journey home from school? Take us there . . .

At the weekends? The school holidays? Parties . . .

Can you write your experience of school . . .

Detail, as always, is key. Think about the squeak of when a trainer hits the sports hall floor, the energy of the corridors at break time, the shrill of the school bell, the smell of the art room, the feeling of cracked paint. Think about the flap of a dusty text book, ink from a pen . . .

Education out of school

School is not our only form of learning and discovery. What other life lessons have you learned along the way? How and where from? Tell us about them! This could be a hobby or an interest or simply life skills.

Life Lessons

Making mistakes is also a really important way to learn, grow and develop. Have you ever been taught a lesson in life? Has something backfired? Have you ever had to learn 'the hard way'? Could you write about it? Did that experience change you? How?

Experience

We also have those life-changing epic moments of wonder that teach us so much through experience. It might be the first time you saw a dancer perform on stage and thought 'WOW, that's what I want to do!'

Can you write about something that blew you away? A show. A book. A piece of art. A game. A beautiful face. A plant. A piece of music. An athlete. A brilliant goal. A rainbow. Maybe you caught a glimpse of a rare species of animal or travelled to another country or saw a shooting star? Something once in a lifetime. You could write it like a review that is going to be published in a magazine, or any way you wish!

Wardrobe

When was the last time you looked at your clothes? Really studied them? (Don't do it if this depresses you, as it sometimes does me.) What does your wardrobe and style say about you? All clothes have

stories. That's why I love shopping second-hand*. Plus, each item of clothing has a story attached. I have found items in pockets of second-hand clothes, like phone numbers on scraps of paper, hair clips, a pocket mirror . . . all reminders that these clothes once belonged to somebody else.

Have you ever thought about your clothes and what they mean?

Where do they come from?

What do they mean to you?

Do you have any stand-out memories attached to your clothes?

Do you have any lucky clothes?

Can clothes have a life of their own?

Your clothes might outlive you . . .
Where will they go?

As an exercise, choose an item of clothing . . . and spend time with it, as if you were a detective. Imagine your eyes are miscroscopes. What does the item look like in terms of colours, textures, patterns? How does it feel? Can you describe its weight, flexibility and structure?

---

* Also because it's much better for the environment, uses less waste and water, is usually fairtrade, is usually cheaper, if it's from a charity shop you're giving money to a worthy cause AND the likelihood of someone showing up to a party in the same dress as you is far less!

Could you describe it plainly as though you were a lost property officer?

Could you describe it persuasively as though you were advertising it?

How does it smell?

When did you last wear it? How did you feel? What happened?

A little deeper . . .

You could do this exercise with an item of clothing that stands out to you, something that is a bit more significant or meaningful, like a dress you wore to a special event, or trousers you wore for a date, a birthday, a prom, a ceremonial outfit, a tie, a hijab, a veil or headscarf, a uniform, a football shirt, something celebratory or a coat that's been handed down from a loved one.

It could be something you wore to a funeral.

Something that reminds you of a difficult time, like what you were wearing on a challenging day or during a moment of shock?

Or embarrassment?

It could be an item of clothing that belonged to a loved one that carries memories.

What have you chosen? Why?

How does it look? Feel? Smell?

How could you write about it?

What memories does the fabric bring up for you?

Do you feel connected to it?

When was the last time you wore it? Saw it worn?

How have you changed since?

How does it make you feel?

Family

When writing about family, I always draw from my own experience, even if I'm writing a completely new fictional character. I always go back to my childhood and my relationship with my siblings. Their characteristics and charms morph, blend and remix into everything I write. The same goes for all my family members. If you feel uncomfortable writing about your birth family or the family you live with, try writing about your chosen family (friends and loved ones).

Here are some prompts to get you going. You can set a timer for a minute or just see what comes . . .

What are your family's habits? (And the habits of individuals in your family . . .)

What are your family's in-jokes?

What don't you agree with a family member(s) about?

What are you grateful to your family for?

Write an average family day in your household.

What songs/TV shows/books remind you of your family?

What colours/textures remind you of your family?

What has your family done for you or how have they made you feel important?

When was the last time you hugged a member of your family? Who was it?

Who do you want to impress in your family?

What would your family say about you?

What has your family taught you?

Is there a challenging time your family went through?

In what ways are you like your family? Or not?

Can you think of a family holiday that stands out? Or a family event/celebration/party?

If there was something you could tell a member of your family, what would it be?

What are you proud of your family for?

How do you think others see your family?

What do you know about your family tree?

That last one in particular could lead to many new roads of inspiration.

Could you write about that?

Other people's families

We've all compared ourselves to other people and other families. I used to have a friend at school whose mum had sewn her name into EVERY item of clothes she owned. From jumpers to socks to swimming costumes to gloves. I was so envious, as though the labelling and manual labour of the sewing itself was a measurement of her mum's love for her. Why didn't MY mum do that for me? Didn't she love me enough to label me with my own name, to claim me as 'taken' with my initials, like I was precious?

Of course I know my mum's love for me is not measured in hand-sewn labels. So this isn't to compare in an unhealthy way but to acknowledge that other families' dynamics and set-ups can help us to reflect on our own. How has our upbringing informed us, shaped us?

Have you ever watched a family interact and engage and thought about your own?

Have you ever thought, I wish I had two mums? Or, I'm so glad my dad isn't that strict? Maybe you wanted a twin or to live with your grandma? Maybe you wished you were allowed more fizzy drinks or to go to bed later? Maybe you wanted your parents to be more sensible and not so wild?

I used to wish I was allowed to swear. For some reason, I thought that meant you had cool parents.

What's coming up for you? Write about it!

Listen to your elders

I was the first child to be born in my parents' friendship group, so I spent a lot of time with adults, up late with them while they drank wine and I sipped Ribena, with an excitement, a curiosity – trying to understand them, work them out. My favourite thing about adults was watching and eavesdropping on their conversations, especially a dinner party or a natter over tea at my neighbour's house (this always meant something dramatic was going on). I think so much of my ambition and desire to be a storyteller was inspired by watching and listening to adults tell stories, real stories, told in their own genuine, authentic way.

Quick, close your eyes (after I've told you what to do) – can you see yourself in a kitchen as a child listening to conversation around you? Who is there? What is going on? What's the atmosphere like? What's for dinner? How do you feel?

We've all seen a grandparent warbling on about 'the good old days' or a teacher going off on an eyeball-rolling tangent about 'when I was at school . . .' We've all done that here-we-go face. But sometimes I'd hear something that was heart-breaking, moving, hilarious, adventurous and inspiring, so, instead of zoning out, I started tuning in. I began to listen actively, as in actually listen. And I began asking questions too! And some really unctuous material oozed out!

Grandparents are a bubbling hotpot of resource and sometimes there are mammoth juicy truffles hidden in their 'good old days' memories! I know we don't all have the luxury of a living grandparent or a close relationship with a grandparent or anybody older, but I've found that talking to adults with experience (who don't mind sharing) to be so helpful when coming up with new ideas.

At ninety-five my nanna is as sharp as a pin; she is a great reader, a fantastic storyteller with a pitch-perfect ear for timing and humour and has an incredible memory – and life! Every time I give my nanna a call – well, firstly, I don't seem to be able to get her off the phone – but after every conversation I come away with my brain bursting with freshly baked ideas cooked by her! I always seem to find out new things about her and her life every time we speak – like that the McDonald's near where she lives used to be a cinema where she dated my pops. Before she told me it was almost impossible to imagine that big white blindingly shiny building as a glitzy cinema, but once she began talking the wallpaper seemed to magically plaster itself onto the walls, the ugly tiled floor changed into a red-velvet carpet and I noticed the four grand pillars – how had I missed them? – holding the front up. Before I knew it, I was tasting the sweet cinema ice cream and seeing my nanna aged nineteen arm-in-arm with my pops.

When my nanna had to say her final 'goodbye' to her own mum (my great-grandmother, who died before I was born), her mum slipped her hands up the cuffs of my nanna's oversized coat, her weak hands gripped her wrists to say goodbye. It was so emotional hearing her speak like this and I knew she appreciated telling me, and I felt privileged being able to hear it.

She tells me so many brilliant stories about my dad when he was small too, which I love because it's difficult to envisage my dad being a little boy. My favourite stories are of her staying at a girls' dormitory during the war, sharing the bathroom, rationing shampoo and sneaking out of the window and down the drainpipes to kiss the cheeky soldiers. And her life with my pops, who has since passed: the time they would be sent bars of chocolate in the post with money hidden inside from relatives and their glamorous parties and dinners.

The same goes for my grandad on my mum's side, who happens to be a historian, architect, author and painter (so you can imagine his knowledge – he's like an encyclopaedia). In five minutes he can light a flame in my brain and new ideas come bursting out of my ears!

Fortunately, both my grandparents love talking to me about their lives. They both love playing the storyteller and I love being the audience. I love two-ways such as this, where they feel satisfied because they are sharing and I am listening, and at the same time I come away feeling inspired and educated, like we've bonded. These stories don't have to go directly into my work but they certainly stoke the fire of creativity; they jostle the rocks and get my imagination going in different directions. It makes for a rich tapestry of storytelling. And, don't forget, their actions might have led to the story of you!

A grown-up you live with is another good place to start too. Once I get my dad going it's like unlocking a labyrinth. He talks of his wild punk days, gigs, parties. He's off: associating names with places (mostly pubs to be fair), reeling off dates and cars and clothes and who was going out with who, from actors to poets to pub crawls and bringing it all back to song lyrics, poems, novels, film, fashion, politics. My mum has unbelievable stories of all the weird, wild and wonderful jobs she's had over the years, from being a comedian to breaking a world record, playing Jane from Tarzan on stage and dancing on TV to being a film director and a mechanic! (Who knew!)

You might find stories from your family members, neighbours, teachers.

Look, I'm not saying be a historian or write autobiographically, but I am saying that stories are everywhere; it's just about tuning in. And what a simple and yet meaningful way to source new (old) material with heart and truth to it.

A great way to begin is by looking at photographs together. When my nanna brings out the leather-bound photo albums, I know it's time to get comfy and go back to a world before me. You'll need to make sure that the stories are handled with care, that everybody is completely comfortable and supported and that you're being a listener not a journalist! And be careful not to steal or hijack their experience or exploit their privacy. If you do feel the need to take notes or record, make sure to check that that's OK with them too. You never know, one day you might be a grandparent yourself who wants to tell a story . . . What story would you tell?

Have you ever pictured yourself older? Where do you see yourself? Who and where would you like to be?

Firsts

Our 'firsts' always stick out in our minds. They are transitions, milestones, and can provoke memory and feelings. For these exercises you can set a timer – try a minute or two for each or free-write. If one really sticks out for you, maybe make it a larger piece of work, and feel free to add your own too!

In no particular order . . .
First pair of shoes
First song I bought/loved
First time I went out on my own (as a child)
First friend
First time I told a lie
First time I had an accident
First time I felt embarrassed
First love
First holiday
First show/gig
First party
First time I . . . (up to you)

You could also use these as first-date questions! Be my guest – see what comes back. The date might not work out but you could come back with some INCREDIBLE new stories to inject into your work!

Little big questions

Have you ever bought yourself some flowers? I have just about managed to buy flowers for the kitchen table (they were on sale and I had a friend coming over), but never for me. It's too easy to put ourselves last. We might see self-compassion and kindness as a luxury. In the hazy wash of life we sometimes forget to listen to who is most important; it's easier to prioritise others, to slam the oxygen mask over the face of a loved one when it's us who are gasping for air.

This is a chance, a magical moment, to listen in to you. I wrote these questions with you in mind but I was thinking about questions I'd quite like to be asked. Spend time on them if you can. If writing about yourself feels like a challenge, then fly through them with a timer . . . but try . . .

What would happen if you sat down, wrapped a toasty blanket round your shoulders and tried to answer these questions . . . ?

When was a time you got what you needed and not what you wanted?

What is your greatest wish?

How could you grow as a person?

What have you overcome?

How have you changed?

Name a time when your reality was not what you had expected.

Think of a time you wished you had said something to someone but never did . . .

What would those words have been? Write them down if you can . . .

When are you at your happiest?

What makes you vulnerable?

What makes you feel safe?

When did you last feel listened to/appreciated/cared for?

What is the kindest thing anybody has ever done for you?

When did you last feel understood?

What are you proud of yourself for?

What do you love about yourself?

When did you last say 'sorry'?

When did you last say 'I love you'?

When was your last proper cuddle and who was it with?

Well done. How do you feel after that?

If you have a character in mind, perhaps you could run through the list for them . . .

Little you

What were you like as a small child? What went through your mind at that age? What did you want? What were you excited about? What were you frightened of? Go with the thoughts, write them down. These can be any fragments and they don't have to make sense.

If any memory jumps out at you, go with it (if you're comfortable to) and see what comes . . .

Could this be the start of a story?

Did you have a favourite toy, teddy or comfort blanket as a child? Could you find it now? If you can, great (no worries if not; you can still do the exercise from memory) . . . How does it feel looking at that toy now? What thoughts and feelings are coming up for you? Could you describe it? Try writing about it without saying what it is? Maybe you can place the toy into a story?

How do you think this toy feels about you? Could you try, just for fun, writing about that?

Can you talk to an adult who knew you as a small child? A family member or friend. Somebody who loves you! Maybe they have a photo album or your first teeth in a jar or a lock of your baby hair they could show you? Maybe a first pair of shoes, a babygrow or blanket? Ask them what you were like as a baby and child. What has changed about you? What behaviours did you do then that you still do now? Did you learn anything new about yourself? Here are some questions you could start asking:

Where was I born?

What was I like as a baby/small child/growing up?

What was my first word?

Are there any particular memories about me that stand out?

What was my favourite book/song/TV show?

What was my favourite food?

You could even put a question to the adult you're talking to: what was it like meeting me for the first time?

More might come from these questions. Think about the story I shared with you about the birth of my son. It can be fascinating to know how we came into the world; you never know, there might be a lot more to your story than you thought.

How does this make you feel?

Can you find a photograph of yourself as a child? Try to really meditate on it. Can you locate the memory?

Where were you?

Who were you with?

Who took the photo?

What can you hear, smell, see?

What is not captured in the photo but there?

What memories do you have from that day?

Plant yourself in the moment and write about it in the first person. Could you try writing in the voice of your younger self?

Try writing from the viewpoint of somebody else, perhaps the photographer or a stranger passing by.

Try writing from the viewpoint of something not human – a tree, a bench, the sky, a jumper.

This might seem like a simple exercise, but you could well be surprised to see what comes out!

Letter writing

Write a letter to little you.

If you could speak to little you, what would you say? Would you warn yourself of anything? Give encouragement? Reassurance? Advice?

I appreciate that it might be tough work, so well done.

If you could write a letter to anyone in your life, telling them something, who would it be to? What would it be about? What would it say?

(You definitely don't have to send it!)

Somebody that I used to know

Friends from primary school, teachers, neighbours, that soul mate you met on holiday that you thought you'd be friends for life with who you never saw again. That person in class who was your Ride or Die and now you barely even acknowledge each other. We've all had these encounters and they mean so much at the time. But then for one reason or another, even with the greatest intentions of keeping close, it didn't work out; grown apart, grown up, moved away, fallen out. Are there any names and faces jumping out to you?

See if you can think about them without searching social media but relying on your own memories. Here some questions to prompt you:

Who is this person?

Where did you meet them?

What stands out about them? Any characteristics? Quirks? Habits? Charms?

Were you close?

What happened?

Why didn't you stay in touch?

Write down any thoughts or feelings . . . any significant moments . . .

Did they teach you anything?

If you saw them now, how would you react? What would you say?

Taking care of future you

Every Christmas my mum gets very stressed. As a proud matriarch with three excitable children (yes, we're adults but, whatever, it's CHRISTMAS), two grandchildren, bazillions of pets and not being the most organised of people, Christmas can be a very heightened time of year! So my mum started writing a letter to herself after the season was over. What went wrong, what went right.

She calls this: **Taking care of future me.**

The letters began with things like not to spend money on pointless presents, not to leave wrapping to the last minute, when to actually put the food in the oven, that she doesn't have to put crosses in the sprouts and the perfect gravy recipe. A reminder to keep away from the mangos! She leaves herself hints and tips, what she bought her in-laws (so she doesn't get them the same present twice) and how to wrap the lights on the tree so they don't knot up when she takes them down. But as time has gone on, Mum has started adding some great pearls of wisdom that have actually served her and benefitted her mental health. Things like: 'remember the kids are tired and overexcited, so don't argue back if they have a tantrum.' (That tantrum bit is OBVIOUSLY not about me.) Or: 'Spend time with the family, not money on things no one needs.' Or: 'Everybody will happily eat beans on toast so don't spend ages in the kitchen.' And: 'Laura always cries at Christmas, don't take it personally.' Er . . . rude.

Sometimes they are just words like 'RELAX' and 'SIT DOWN' and 'DON'T FORGET TO ENJOY IT'.

Then she hides the letter in the cardboard box with the Christmas-tree decorations, which she opens in early December. She says they are the best present she ever gave herself.

A letter to your future self

If you could talk to your future self, what would you say? Write a letter (or email) to yourself to read in a year's time – it doesn't have to mark a special occasion or anniversary. You can write anything you'd like.

Put a stamp on it, post it and when it arrives on your doormat, DON'T open it – resist the temptation (you know what it says anyway) and put it away in a drawer somewhere safe. Set a reminder on your phone for this very day in exactly a year – and then you can open it . . .

Fears

I wrote lots about fear in my memoir. Of course this was ironic, as I was so scared of writing about fear in the first place. But the illness made me interrogate fear. What made me scared and for what reason?

I wrote about fear deliberately. Why? Because I am a scaredy-cat. I was doing this to be mean to myself. I wanted to view my threats and fears realistically. I wrote a long list of things that scared me. I made sure I was completely honest and didn't hold back, no matter how ridiculous or unique or silly they sounded. I made sure to include the big ones with the small ones too, treating all of them with equal 'respect'.

Here are some of my fears (they come from a very long list) in no particular order:

Ghosts
Witches
Zombies
The dark
Being left out by my friends

Hills/ramps/slopes

Streatham (don't ask!)

After I had recovered my fears changed. What had once scared me no longer did now my perspective had changed.

Here are some things that scare me now, in no particular order:

My family breaking apart

Not being able to use my imagination

Being afraid of my own mind

Getting unwell again

And, of course, as a mum I have worries about my child too.

But even with all these fears, I can challenge and rationalise them to a degree with CBT (Cognitive Behavioural Therapy). I am able to live alongside them.

Write a list of all your fears and why you think you have them. Have they changed in any way?

Why do you think we experience fear?

What makes you happy?

In the same way, what makes you happy? I love hearing the pure everyday things that make people happy – ice cream, family, holidays, a pet, books . . .

What makes YOU happy? Actually HAPPY? Not anybody else, you. For example, for many years of my life I pretended I loved camping at outdoor festivals because my friends enjoyed it. YAY! I'M SO HAPPY BEING OUTDOORS, COLD AND WET WITH ALL THE WORMS! No, I don't like it. To me, camping is uncomfortable. I want a proper shower. A toilet that flushes and a real mug of tea. I don't like sleeping on the floor. I don't like weeing in grass. I don't like that horrible feeling of waking up feeling like you've been wrapped in cellophane. Call me a diva, I don't care. And it feels liberating saying that out loud. Thank you for listening.

What about you? It could be as simple as TV. Perfecting a cartwheel? A new pen? Getting your hair just right? Matching socks? When your train is on time. When you hear your favourite song. Bumping into a friend. When your team scores. Being with someone you love . . .

We think it's the big things that make us happy but it isn't, is it? For me it really is all about those little things . . .

Here are some of my favourite little things that make me happy and give me an inner glow: flipping my pillow to the cold side in the middle of the night, running in the rain, picking melted cheese off the side of the lasagne dish, hot buttery toast, the moment the lights go down in the theatre and everyone goes quiet, fresh pyjamas, singing in the car, giving somebody a present, being with my family, my first cup of tea in the morning, watching cooking programmes, my son's laugh . . .

Write your list, maybe adding why. Be as detailed as possible.

Seven

JUST WRITE IT

Flex. Have fun. Run with it.

Well done. You've made it this far. Now it's time for you to flex. Have fun. Run into it. Go for it. Dig deep. Get out of your head and on to the page. Think about everything we've covered: remembering that inspiration is everywhere, that there's no such thing as a bad idea, to trust your instinct and go with your gut, that bad writing doesn't exist, that the first mark is not for ever. Remember that you can chop and change and edit and restructure later. That you can scratch out and improve. Keep with you that you are important, that you are interesting, that detail and the senses are precious, that your story is enough. Remember to try not to sound like anybody else, to write how you talk, to float past the inner critic. That you never need to show a soul if you don't want to. That all you need is your brain and your heart. That is all.

Don't give up. I will be here the whole time with you, holding your hand, cheering from the sidelines or simply watching you in awe! Ready and waiting to applaud you at the other side and so just write IT. Just write IT. IT. You know what IT is. You know where IT lives, what IT looks like, where IT sits, how IT moves. How IT hides, how IT shifts. How long IT stays, if IT ever leaves. Where IT breathes. And only you know that. And IT knows that too. Where does IT come from? Does IT creep up on you? How do you control IT? What do you say to IT? How do you feel about IT? What is IT?

If you are struggling to get started, here are some very open prompts that you can apply to an experience or story you might like to write about.

What happened?

Does it hurt? If so, where does it hurt?

Do you keep this feeling/emotion in your body? If so, where does it live?

What are your memories?

Can you write down any visuals? Colours, shapes, sounds?

How does/did it feel?

Did you learn anything?

What do you want to say?

Or if they don't work for you, keep reading . . . Just be. That's absolutely fine.

Eight

TO WRITE AND KEEP WRITING

Writing for yourself is self-care and an act of self-kindness.

We don't always have to have an end goal in mind. The aim here is not to 'get published', to see our book in a bookshop, to turn our script into a blockbuster, hear our song on the radio or do recital in a cafe. Writing for yourself is self-care and an act of self-kindness.

If you do want to continue writing, if you are finding it helpful, fun, therapeutic, cathartic or relaxing, here are some more ideas of how to keep it up.

Practical things to try to write about

If the well of inspiration is ever running on empty, if life has become static or tired, if you need a break from a larger project that might need some resting time, you need a distraction or just need a refresh, here are some cool practical ideas to keep things moving, how to maintain your writing six-pack and keep your imagination fed and your your creativity pumping.

Be instinctive, responsive, honest and natural.

Go for a walk/run/cycle – write about it.

Put on a song and sing out loud – write about it.

Call a friend – write about it.

Cook – write about it.

Do something that's needed doing for a long time that you've put off, like fixing something or posting something or sorting out clothes – then, you guessed it, write about it.

Reach out to somebody you've been meaning to – write about it.

Go to a gallery or museum – write about it.

Go and hang out with nature – write about it.

Go to the library – write about it.

If not too uncomfortable for you, go to a graveyard – write about it.

Do something fearless, something brave – write about it.

Go swimming – write about it.

Go ice skating, go-karting, bowling (the shoes, ohhhhh, the shoes) – write about it.

Beauty in the mundane, domestic and everyday

Not everything needs flamboyance and theatre. It doesn't always need to be snowy mountains, fire-breathing dragons, sword fights, shipwrecks, affairs, car crashes and murder. Sometimes we think our stories aren't enough as they are. We feel the need to include drama to up the stakes. There's a temptation to make all our leads look like Hollywood actors with straight white teeth and give everybody a really 'cool' and 'interesting' name. Well, there is beauty here in real life; there is so much to pull from the everyday, and the truth is: if you're looking to share your work, most readers will relate to your story if they see themselves inside it. Most readers are looking for an 'ah, yes' moment or a 'me too' moment. It's about empathy, relatability and connection. So, yes, write fantasy, write abstract and surreal – but never forget a magic sprinkle of the mundane.

You are enough. You are interesting. Tell your story. That is all there is.

Use the news

You are documenting the human experience. Absorbing and living in this almighty, beautiful, ever-changing, terrifyingly gorgeous, hopeful chaos; there are loads of things to be mad about. Sad about. Confused about. Scared about. There's loads to love too. How do you react and respond to what's going on around you? How do the times we live in impact our creativity? Day-to-day life?

Write down some thoughts. You could track your findings with a diary, start a conversation with your writing . . . ask questions.

If you find the news and current affairs overwhelming, confusing or panic-inducing (I know I do) and you prefer to live in a bubble, write about that too. Why is that? What is your bubble?

You couldn't write it

Newspapers and magazines are great ways to find stories. I once read a story about a man who washed up on a shore in a full suit – he even had a carnation in his top pocket. He couldn't remember how or why he got there but explained that he was expected to be at a piano recital. This was a real life story but it also felt like the start of a story.

I remember another about a man who found a whole rat in his tin of beans.

From the reunion of long-lost family members, lottery winners, miracle survivors, pets saving their owners' lives, to ghost stories and grandparents who celebrate their 100th birthday, the newspaper can be a deep well of ideas. Newspaper stories are not always dark and harrowing. Often they can be heartwarming, hilarious or completely silly. I'll never forget my favourite – a burglar who got caught burgling a family home because the dad of the family told a joke and the burglar laughed out loud. I mean, how good is that?

As we mentioned earlier, travel magazines can be so inspiring for places you haven't been, covering everything from landscape, culture and food. Ones with photographs are even more enticing. National Geographic is also the most wonderfully inspiring magazine for a broader picture of the world, with beautiful photography and dazzling writing. Old second-hand editions are also usually easy to come by.

Estate agents' windows and catalogues are also useful for finding new locations. This is a great way to flesh out real-life stories but can also spark intrigue and mystery and germinate new settings.

I used to endlessly dream about the house I'd live in when I grew up. Sometimes it was a ginormous mansion palace, other times it would be a crumbly twee little cottage in the middle of nowhere, or a terracotta cave in the Mediterranean. I used to draw maps of my future homes; I'd spend ages designing the blueprint of the imaginary layout with huge indoor/outdoor gardens, pizza ovens, butterfly houses, roaming peacocks, fruit trees. Inside: jacuzzis, a library, a cinema room, a huge walk-in wardrobe, a ballroom with a giant twirling disco ball.

What would your future house look like?

Sometimes we don't play out these dreams that live in our heads because we fret that we'll look silly. Well, it's silly not to be silly. We are humans, we are inventors and dreamers. We need to explore our fantasies; LET US LIVE!

Tips to keep you writing

Writing is different to playing a sport, where once the game is done so are you – you win, you lose or you draw – and you can relax until you want to play again. Or weaving a blanket, where the results are consistant, clear and evident for all to see. With writing it isn't always obvious how far you've come. Some days are great. Others not so easy.

You might be tempted to delete whole chunks of your work, throw your words or plans away, not show anybody, start again or give up entirely. But don't. Nothing is a waste. Writing and using your imagination creatively is good for your soul. Even if you can't see the results, they are there. They are in you. Trust the process. And yourself.

Write like you mean it

Write like you mean it, all the time, in everything you do. Recognise that your words have power and strength – and I don't mean that all your writing needs to be worthy and serious. It can be silly, funny and off the wall too. But from text messages and emails to shopping lists and notes left on the fridge – write as yourself. Use YOUR words, new words, be characterful, charming, heartfelt. Imagine that one day, when you're long gone, everything you ever wrote will be placed in a museum. Wouldn't you want everything to sound like you, to come from a place of intention? Wouldn't you want your smile to translate? Your tears to be felt through the words? Your personality to shine through?

Have a go and watch how this simple addition to your everyday life will close the gap between yourself and your writer self.

Welcome interruptions

There is a misconception that writers need complete silence and solitude for 'good writing'. Sure, we all have to concentrate, and if you are surrounded by chaos you aren't going to get much writing done. But I sometimes feel that if I waited for the peace and quiet, I'd never get any writing done at all ever (maybe it's the same for you!). Have you ever tried leaning in to the chaos? Life is full of interruptions. We are constantly being woken from our consciousness by somebody or something – a phone call, a text message, a doorbell ringing, a baby crying or the washing machine finishing, or somebody calling our name. Life interrupts us all the time. There is a way to write inside and around that fuzzy noise of life and see the interruptions as gear switches, which can get us writing outside our comfort zones.

When writing realism, interruptions can be useful. Just as an experiment, the next time you are interrupted during your writing, don't panic or be annoyed by it, but see if this prompts you to play around with your writing and take it in a new direction.

Anyway, not all interruptions are bad. Sometimes there's nothing better than a gentle rap on the door and to be handed a cup of tea.

Feed your head

Do stuff, see stuff, read stuff, eat stuff, talk about stuff with friends and family and strangers. Use your hands, use your legs, use your body, use your face. Dream, be silly, have fun, ask questions, get out there, stay in, have a sleep, stay awake, watch that, do that, get on that, get off that, go out, look up there, look down there and over there, open the windows, let in the air, wear that, say yes to something new, choose life. Say no to something that you've been plucking up the guts to say no to too. If somebody challenges you and asks you why, say 'because I'm writing' – or 'because I'm floating', 'because I'm dreaming', 'because I'm busy', 'because I don't need a reason. But thanks.' Be courageous, say that thing, take your time, unscrew the lid, question, question, question, open this, close that, take a minute, climb a mountain, open your eyes, open your mind, have a go. Just try . . .

Everything is relevant.

You are not the only thing

Do you reckon an ant thinks it's the only thing? Do you suppose a slug thinks it's the star of its own stage show? We are not the only thing but sometimes we think we are. The cameras turn inwards and we can't see outside. Our perspective morphs. **It is not all about us.** But when life is intensified, say, on our birthday or if we're going through something tough, we might forget that it is not all about us. You are not being singled out. You are not being targeted. You are not being chosen. You are not the only gift to this Earth. You are not a martyr. You are not a scapegoat. This isn't harsh; this is comforting if you think about it. It turns the volume down. It takes off the pressure. If I make a mistake, I find it important to remind myself that it's not a big deal. That it's not the end of the world. That millions of mistakes are being made all over the world all day long and, look, the Earth is still the Earth. It's part of life. There are bigger things going on. Time will pass. Things will change. It is important to sometimes remind ourselves that we are small. That we are a part of something greater.

Here are some ways to help remind yourself . . .

Make friends with a tree

I am just not joking. Make friends with a big tree. Plant your feet right up by its roots. Admire its life, its age, its presence, its stillness, its grace. Isn't it beautiful? What can you learn about it? What can you learn from it? What has it seen? What does it hear? What does it know? Touch its bark. Admire its leaves. Respect its growth. Isn't it magnificent? Give your tree a name if you want, but don't expect it to come to Nando's with you, soz.

Wow, the big old sky

You know how kids draw the sky as one big blue line across the top of the page? Isn't that cute? When you think about the sky it's difficult to know where it starts and where it stops. It's all over us and all around us, everywhere and nowhere – and yet we point up, don't we? When we get older, we know that the sky is not just a line at the top; it's above us, yes, but it immerses us in it too. Lie down flat on your back, find a patch of sky where you can see all of it, the whole sky uninterrupted, and now look up – huge, open and vast. See how it eats you up, see how it's all you can see, take it in. Breathe in cold air, breathe out tired old air, and remind yourself that we are all under the same sky ON A PLANET THAT IS HANGING IN THE SKY. YES I KNOW, WHAT THE HELL? Try not to let that scare you – let it comfort you. We are all in this, all of us.

> Can you write about the sky? Track the sky's changes? Capture it? Can you see clouds? Texture? Colours? Density?
>
> How is the sky used to colour in a story?

The actual moon, man

LOOK AT THE MOON. That big silver eyeball watching you from the window. Is it your friend? If the moon could talk, what would it say? How does it feel? Have you ever spoken to the moon? Who is your moon?

Is it somebody in your life who always has an eye on you? Someone you can depend and rely on? Someone you look up to? A guardian who makes you feel safe and secure?

Maybe it reminds you of someone you've lost?

Looking at the moon is a great way to feel small, to remind yourself we are a part of something, the same as the grass, the bugs, the Earth!

As an experiment, maybe you could get to know the moon a bit? Log its changes, its appearances. When does the moon look scary, happy or 'Halloween-y' werewolf or Dracula-like? When is it as transparent as glass or misty? When is it crescent-shaped? Golden? Silver? Red? Blue?

You could use some moontalk in your writing to show off your poetry skills!

The moon is symbolic, especially when it comes to mental health and mental illness. In loneliness, loss and love, there's the idea that you can be underneath the same sky and yet separated from someone you care about. How is the moon used in literature?

The sun

The sun and moon are often referred to as total opposites. In folklore they are lovers that never meet or relatives that have been separated at birth. In *Romeo and Juliet*, Shakespeare describes the lovers as like the sun and moon.

We think of the sun as a yellow or orange circle in the sky shining down on us when really it is, oh, just a HOT BALL OF GLOWING GASES! What the hell does that even mean? What do you think?

How do people change when the sun is shining?

We always associate the sun with happiness. But how does the sun make you feel? How can it be used to influence your writing?

You can think about things like a lovely long stretched-out hot summer's day, the way the sun dances on skin, the way the sun bleaches the posters on your bedroom wall . . . and how does the sunlight come in through a window? What words comes up for you?

Get cosmic

You might have heard phrases like 'written in the stars' or 'starcross'd lovers' or the John Green book *The Fault in Our Stars*. Stars, planets and space are mythical and mysterious. They are an explosive way of exploring themes like fate, destiny and legacy. They are also a wonderful way in for writing new material or adding some spicy poetic, metaphorical language into your work. Astronomy has always been an experimental way to tell stories, to reflect and explore. Suspend superstition and play with the star signs, constellations, the stories of stars. There is a whole other universe happening over our heads – this could be a cool way to ignite ideas for you and create some magic on the page. I'm not saying fork out on an impressive telescope, but googling images won't hurt.

What can you see?
How does it look?
How does it make you feel?
What are the stories behind our stars?

To infinity . . .

I remember once CRYING, as in ACTUALLY crying, in a science lesson at secondary school because I hadn't ever really thought about what was 'beyond' space. When my physics teacher quite simply replied 'infinity' his answer just didn't seem to answer my MASSIVE question. Infinity. So just for ever? What does that mean? What does that look like? How long is 'for ever'? The abyss, the stars, the planets – the existential endlessness that is bigger than we could ever imagine.

But if it does feel OK, have you thought about it? Have you ever tried to write about that? To put it into words?

Is there another life out there? Do you think there is a version of you on another planet?

And, of course, beyond . . .

Have you asked yourself what is beyond space? Have you ever talked with family and friends about it?

Why we are here?

What is this all for?

What's the meaning of life?

I think it's important to think about life in its power, mightiness, hugeness, vastness and volcanic velocity so that we are able to put things into perspective. It is healthy to be curious, to wonder, to interrogate, explore and get philosophical. And 'writing' is a perfect arena to thrash out these thoughts.

What happens after 'life'? No, really, what happens? Where do you think we go?

None of this is to trigger an existential crisis that means you have to have a day off to hide under the blanket on your bed; these are purely questions to spur ideas and thoughts, to inspire some cool new writing and germinate ideas. Don't take anything too seriously. If anything feels too big, float past it, or do the warming-up technique from page 241.

Water

Water is everything. Water is EVERYTHING. You are made of water. I am made from water. We need it to live; we need it to survive. Water is so inspiring. Here are some water exercises to get your writing flowing just like it . . .

Have you ever heard of water expressed as being something challenging, like 'troubled waters'?

We think of water as a danger, a threat, a journey, but also it can be a baptism, a cleanse, a wash-over, a restart. Sure, there can be stormy seas but there can also be purity.

Can you think of how water is used in songs, literature, cinema and art to show emotion?

We can learn a LOT from water. It is a beautiful metaphor for the ebb and flow of life and is used to death in writing – and yet somehow it never gets old.

Try to get near some flowing water (safely!) and experience it up close. A stream. A babbling brook. A river. A lake. The ocean. A canal.

Notice how you can never capture running or flowing water. As soon as you do, it becomes still. If we are to have a flowing life packed with change, discovery and adventure, we need to let it flow . . .

Write about the colours, sounds, textures, depth and movement of water.

What rhythm and patterns do you notice?

How does it reflect light and images?

Why do people and wildlife flock to water?

What does water make you think about?

How does it make you feel?

Find still water – a pond, a swimming pool, even a puddle will do or, failing that, fill a sink and take a look.

What colours are you seeing? Shapes? Surfaces?

How does it make you feel?

What does it make you think of?

Write about it.

If you are able to swim, how does that feel? How does it feel to feel weightless?

Look for water. On the ground. On leaves, dewdrops. In the air. How does it land on cars, the road, clothes and skin? How does it mist?

What about steam? Even from a pan of water, the kettle, the shower (but please take care).

Condensation – what can you write on glass?

And what about ice? Can you write about ice?

Put a block of ice on your tongue and let it melt. Write about it.

Put a block of ice in your mouth and crunch it down to shards. Write about it.

Thaw?

Frost?

How does water affect clothes and fabrics – wool, silk, fleece, cotton? What happens? How does their weight and texture change? How do these materials dry?

How does water affect hair? Feathers? Bread? Wood? Metal?

Notice how bridges are used in artistic expression as metaphors for peace, forgiveness, hope and love, crossing dangerous water.

How can you use these experiments in your writing? To strengthen a scene of somebody getting caught in the rain? Or swimming in the ocean to find a pearl? Or a pirate sailing the seas or a mermaid's hair? How could you use your own pan of boiling pasta to demonstrate a blocked feeling? Or splashes of water shaken from a dog to show joy?

We don't mess with the bloody sea

If you are able, get to the sea and safely spend some time with it. When was the last time you went and had a look at the sea? Listened to it crashing down and throwing its weight around, wrestling with its boundlessness like a rabid beast or slow and shushing, all lullaby-dreamy and calm? See how you know, instinctively, that the water is BOSS. YOU DON'T MESS WITH THE SEA.

We respect the sea; we know it could kill us, swallow us completely. Why is that? How does the sea feel on our skin? Why do we believe it to be blue or green? Hold it in your hands – what colour is it now? Does the sea sing? How does the sea make you feel? See how people gather near water? What has the sea seen? What does it know? Does it make you feel calm? Does it make you feel angry? Does it make you feel happy? Peaceful? Reflective? Do you feel like you want to jump in or does it intimidate you? Do you feel like you have an understanding with it? How does the sea change our mindset?

The sea is often used in poetry, song lyrics and fiction to describe moods and relationships. I've used it myself. We all know that feeling like we're 'caught in a storm' or a 'shipwreck', that there are 'stormy seas ahead' or the 'calm' before or after 'the storm' or experiencing the 'wind' being taken from our 'sails'. That we're 'drowning', that we might need 'rescuing'. Why do you think that is? Can you relate?

Sailing, journeying and travelling is a fantastic visual for the story of life. *The Old Man and the Sea* or *Life of Pi* are wonderful examples of this. We're told we're the 'captains' of our ships and I've often felt 'compassless' and like I'm against the elements. Is there a time in your life where you've felt you've been 'stuck' or 'lost' at sea or caught in the 'eye of the storm'?

We also know the phrase 'smooth' or 'plain' sailing . . . What does that mean to you . . . ?

What would your paradise island look like? Who would be there? What would be there? Could you live there for ever?

A glass of water

Fill a glass of water and sit with it. Does it change? Write about it.

Pour the water into another glass. Fill glasses, bottles and containers, and mix the water with oil. See how it separates? Write about it.

Muddle the water with paint – a little at first. How does it change, cloud, mystify and surprise?

Add ink to water – what happens?

Mix water with flour. Water with washing-up liquid. Water with coffee granules, sugar, tea.

Fill a balloon with water, a carrier bag.

See things float.

See how water can wash us away, swirl us down the drain.

Have a lovely bath – a big one right up to the top with bubbles – really go in, treat yourself. Go on then, throw in a bath bomb. What did you think about while you were in the bath? How did you feel? When was the last time you did that? (That's not an exercise, that's just for you, but tell whoever you live with that it's really important homework that simply CANNOT wait.)

What do you think about in the shower?

Have a freezing-cold shower. How long can you stand it?

When you drink water, how do you feel?

How does water taste? Some people say it tastes of nothing. Nice answer, but I don't think that's true. How does 'nothing' taste to you? Write about it.

Is there actually a better feeling than water when you're really thirsty?

Think about all the things that rely on water every single day.

Think about how fortunate we are to have clean water running from our taps. Can you write about that?

What 'colour' is water?

How does water feel on your skin?

What memories are coming up for you?

Fire

Every time I sit in front of a fire I go into a daydream. My face relaxes, my jaw slackens and my tongue becomes loose. I feel ready to talk and ready to listen. I become completely transfixed by the dancing flames, the flicking fingers, the licking tongues of the golden and amber and orange hands. Humans are drawn to fire for survival – for warmth, to cook food, for light, for safety and community – but see how we build round fire. How a fireplace is a centrepiece in a home, how a fire is the base of a camp. How fire can be an evening trick of theatre, transforming us, inviting us to tell stories, sing songs and share secrets. That's why in a cowboy film the fire moment is always that confessional deep moment where the silent hero speaks their sentimental truth . . . It's elemental, raw, pure magic. But also, it's a focus point, something to 'look' at when opening up, which protects us from feeling exposed or judged, so we don't have to look each other in the eyes. That's why it's easier to have big conversations in the car or when taking a long walk rather than sitting opposite each other at the table. Where do you have your big conversations? What about your friends and members of your family? Your writing could be a similar place to open up without feeling exposed or judged. This can be your fire.

> Light a candle and watch the flame. See how it moves and morphs, see how even the smallest of flames is completely alive and spirited? BE CAREFUL with fire, of course. And check with an adult first.
>
> How does it make you feel?
>
> How do you feel about the heat?
>
> How does it compare with your mood and emotions?
>
> What does fire make you think of?
>
> Have you ever really thought about how fire is created?
>
> Can you write about fire without telling us what it is?
>
> If fire was a character, who would it be?

Weather

The same goes for the weather. The weather is always used as a poetic comparison for our moods and emotions. Sometimes when our moods are all over the place, we wish we had a forecast.

How does the weather change our mood?

Have you ever noticed changes in the way you feel when the weather turns, for better or worse?

We could say we are having a 'sunny' day or that someone has a 'sunny' personality. Maybe you're writing a character with a 'stormy' personality or someone who's caught in a 'red mist'? We could say someone was feeling 'clouded' or 'foggy'. I mean, I definitely felt like I was lost in a fog when I was unwell. And when I was getting better, I remember the doctor offering hopefully that the 'fog was lifting' or 'clearing'. And we use rainbows to signify hope . . .

How can we use weather metaphorically when writing? And how does weather play a part in our writing? How can it set the tone? How can the temperature of the outside world influence the temperature inside our writing?

Weather can impact our characters' destinies and fortune. Maybe your character is on track but the weather has other ideas? How can we use the weather as a device or tool to simmer scenes or cool them down? To contrast, complement and contradict? It's no surprise that clichéd romance scenes happen in the 'heat of summer' or sad goodbye romance scenes in the snow. Dramatic scenes take place in the rain or a thunderstorm and a writer could be extra manipulative if they want us to feel sorry for a character, by making them walk home, getting absolutely soaked, in the rain . . .

When I was unwell it was spring in London. Usually at this time of year the buds would be bursting out, the blossom trees would be flowering in white, pink and coral and the days would be getting a little bit longer . . . Well, not that year. OUT OF NOWHERE a horrendous freak storm hit in the form of a 'deep depression' called Storm Emma. It seemed so ironic because that's what I felt like inside my head, that what was happening outside was happening to me inside my head. It was as if everything, including the seasons, was overtaken by this great force and the universe was spun out of control. It was like I was trapped in one of those snow globes and an evil giant had picked me up and shaken my world frantically, snow spiralling everywhere, my life upside down.

Weirdly, one of the nurses who treated me back to health had the same name as the storm. I know it's just a coincidence, but these details can make for excellent beats when it comes to storytelling. We call these little breadcrumbs 'Easter eggs'; they're hidden gems to help build and develop our stories, like dropping clues to signpost our reader. It can also be great for comic timing.

Have there been times when the weather has impacted on something in your life?

Can you think of a time the weather has gone along with your mood?

We all know the phrase 'rain on my parade', but have you ever felt like the weather has been on your side or gone against you?

Have you ever experienced a sudden change in weather? Sunny blue skies one minute and a thunderstorm the next, and everyone is running for shelter?

Writing about the weather is a skill in itself. It sounds easy but trying to actually write about snow or rain or a clear sunny day is harder than you think!

Have a go. You could jot down words and emotions or play around with writing about different types of weather. You could reopen a piece you're currently working on and introduce some weather to give a scene more impact, enhance the drama or provoke action or tension. Or simply see what comes.

Here are some ideas . . .

Rain	A storm	Mist
Snow	Wind	Hail
Sunshine	Fog	

Here are some harder ones . . .

Summer rain	Slush	Sleet

That feeling before a storm when the air feels tight and close and the sky feels low

A rainbow

What about the seasons? I feel fortunate to live in the UK where we get a bit of everything. The bouncing weightless boom of spring, the thick warm lick of summer, the everchanging banquet of autumn, and the winter – sometimes as hard and harsh as a scene from *Game of Thrones*, then at other times . . . well . . . just pure elegance.

Maybe this time can you try to write in as much detail as you can about . . . ?

Spring

Summer

Autumn

Winter

Does opening your writing with a specific month or season inform the mood of the reader? I think it might. How can we use that to our advantage or make a character or reader work harder to get round that?

Try to log your own mood with the weather. We all know the feeling of much-needed sun on our skin after days of rain – how does it feel for you?

Get high

NOT LIKE THAT, thank you. Standing at the top of a huge building is not my idea of a good time, but I'll experience heights because I know it's valuable for my writing and living. How can you 'get high'? By climbing a hill? Standing on a bridge or tower? Climbing a building? You don't need to get up very high to experience a change of perspective. Honestly, standing on a small stool does it for me!

Maybe you're going in an aeroplane soon, which can be INCREDIBLE for writing – getting a bird's-eye view of the world can mean the universe begins to look like a board game. Think about when you go somewhere hot and see all the swimming pools like little blue boxes. How do you think you would look now to somebody overhead on a plane? They probably wouldn't even see us, would they?

How do you think the world looks to a bird flying overhead?

Maybe you're good at climbing trees or have a cliff, mountain or pier near you? How does it make you feel to be high?

What does the sensation of height do to our minds and bodies?

Do you feel dizzy? Do you get butterflies? Vertigo? What other experiences could give us this heightened feeling when our feet are on the ground? Love? Excitement? Fear? Surprise? Too many coffees? A sugar rush?

Animals

We can learn SO much from animals.

You might have heard the positive-inspo quote 'Live like a kitten', which in short means:

Eat when you're hungry.

Sleep when you're tired.

And play.

As basic as that sounds, I think there is a lot of wisdom in this.

Animals can also be incredibly beneficial for our health and well-being. Look, I'm not suggesting you go out and immediately adopt a fourteen-year-old bulldog named Agnes (she is cute, though), but animals can be wonderful company. They can be soothing and reassuring, they can be calming to stroke and cuddle, they are fantastic listeners, they don't ask anything more from you than love (and treats), they can help us to keep a routine and trips outside. They encourage us to live.

Animals don't fret about or fear the future like us humans do. They experience reality in the moment; they deal with it practically and then they move on. Animals don't waste their energy worrying about what others will think. A moose isn't concerned about whether a meerkat thinks his antlers are cool. You don't catch a deer at the waterhole having a panic attack about 'what if a wolf comes?' or 'what if the water runs out?'

Animals live in the moment instinctively.

You can learn more about fight-or-flight responses properly from an actual professional if you experience anxiety or panic attacks (I've had two before and they were horrendous), but here are some cool exercises to do that can keep us calm and open our minds, allowing us to admire and learn from animals – and bugs too. Spiders are my best.

Can you think of an experience with an animal or insect? It could be the time a fox looked at you with glistening marble eyes, a cuddle with a hamster, playing with a puppy or an afternoon spent trying to chase a wasp out of the living room . . .

Have you ever felt looked at or understood or heard by an animal? Have you ever bonded with an animal?

When was the last time you held an animal? Stroked or petted one?

If you go outside, how soon is it until you spot an animal or insect? I can see a white butterfly at the window as I write this. I know there are ants on the street outside as they've been there for days, and lime-green parakeets in the park, and geese. Start paying attention to the animals around you, the wildlife you share a planet with.

What was your favourite animal as a child and why? (Mine was a pig because they are cute, funny and apparently incredibly intelligent. My dad used to take us to a pub where two spotted pigs called Salt and Pepper lived in the garden that we could pet and stroke. I thought we were the luckiest kids in the world to know pigs!)

How do you feel about animals?

If you live with an animal – lucky you – you might find this task simpler . . . Study an animal. How does it move, walk, sleep, eat, drink?

Animals can't talk but they can definitely communicate. I grew up with pets so I know that on the whole: dogs yawn when they are stressed and wag their tails when they are excited. Cats pad their paws when they are looking to get cosy, their hairs go on end and they curve their backs when they feel intimidated. Goldfish slink to the bottom of their tanks when they are feeling unhappy or lonely (trust me – and, NO, I DON'T WANT TO TALK ABOUT IT).

Choose one animal or a few or mix it up. Set a timer for a minute or two and blast through it. How does an animal show they are . . .?

Hungry	Sleepy
Happy	Jealous
Scared	Relaxed
Excited	In the mood to play
Concerned	Stressed

I used to look into my dog's big, kind soft brown eyes, right in, as though I was seeing the soul of him, and just think, wow, you're so innocent. You've not hurt one single person today. You're just going about living your dog life. How cool is that?

Words, as we know, are powerful things. What can we say without talking?

How can animals mirror us?

What are animals thinking?

What do they think about us?

Sometimes I imagine that they must think 'these humans are so weird. Slow down and stop running around trying to do everything. Stop trying to please everybody all the time. Just eat and chill, boy. Fart out loud, who cares?'

Other times I think they must think we're stupid! Like the modern world has made us lose all our natural instincts. They must think we're so lazy!

Have animals adapted to the modern world? How have they? And what about the future?

Could you live like an animal for the day and write about it?

We can learn a lot about animals in literature and film. You might see techniques used through the silent mystical 'language' of an animal that signpost us towards clues or showcase character. You might be familiar with animals' loyalty to their owners, even if their owner is a villain.

Or you might have seen it in films or read a scene in a book when a witch walks into a scene and a cat hisses. Or an alien lands in a 'nice neighbourhood' and a dog barks aggressively. We see vampires turn into black birds like crows or ravens or a spray of bugs. Cats, birds, snakes and spiders are often used to represent witchcraft. Wolves are linked to fairy-tales. Rabbits with magic, 'madness' or adventure.

What animals can you think of that are used symbolically as metaphors, to strengthen scenes or add to plot?

How can you flip the script, break an animal's stereotype to thunderbolt new energy into your material to create humour and twists – you could have a lion that is scared, a serious chimpanzee rather than a cheeky one, or an evil fluffy chinchilla!

Fictional animal characters are so important; they can be used as devices to say a lot about a person. You might want to set up a character as mean and selfish and greedy but write a scene in which they give their last bite of sandwich to a hungry street dog – what does that tell us about them? Does it show us another side to them? You might want to show a character who is trying to be nice but then a seagull embarrasses them by stealing their ice cream or pooing on their head, which reveals who they truly are by showing how they react. Can you introduce animals into your writing? Have fun with character and their inner beasts too.

The animal in us

Can you give an animal human qualities and characteristics? For example, could you give a crocodile the personality of your uncle? Could you give a hamster the qualities of your teacher?

And what about the other way round? They always say humans look like their pets. What animals do people you know remind you of? I always say my partner is a sloth, because he's so chilled – he manages to make a bed anywhere out of anything and fall asleep. He also sleeps hanging off the bed.

The animal in you

What animal are you and why?

When writing about ourselves as animals we are often more bold in celebrating the animalistic parts of us that are red-blooded, pure, natural and primal without apology. Writing about ourselves in this raw way can shed some new light on our feelings. For example, when I was afraid I could definitely relate to the 'rabbit in a headlights' type of fear.

In hospital I likened myself to a 'caged tiger' stalking, being hungry like a 'wolf' or a 'pregnant cat' or 'roaring rhino'. There is something the animal has over us humans, which is that they really don't care what people think. And that is something we could pinch a bit from.

Has there ever been a time you've felt animalistic?

Animals as friends and companions

Animals, as you may know, are incredible side-kicks and allies. Think of Sikes's Bulls-eye in *Oliver Twist*. You only have to watch a Disney film to see that nearly every princess or prince has a little animal buddy pal or has an encounter with an animal. One of the most amazing things about these friendships is the lack of judgement. There is a beautiful therapy dog in R. J. Palacio's *Wonder* called Daisy. The protagonist, Auggie, writes how Daisy never judges his appearance – unlike everybody else. Animal friendship and loyalty is very inspiring and makes us adults appear pitiful in comparison. That's why dogs are often referred to as a human's best friend.

These 'silent' companions see it all, stick by us and listen. They remain by our side. Sometimes these friendships outlive human relationships (in both lifespan and depth!). Maybe you've experienced or witnessed relationships like this. I've had friends who have grieved their lost pets as though they were human beings. Have you? Were you given the space you needed to grieve?

> Maybe, if not too upsetting, you could try writing about this experience? Or write about how much you loved your pet. What were they like? This might bring up some fond memories.

Animals can teach us a lot about life and death and what it means to truly be alive. I mean, I saw my cat give birth in an airing cupboard and it was the most wild, graceful and mind-boggling thing I've ever seen.

Has an animal ever taught you anything?

Do they remind you to be kinder to yourself? Do they remind you to LIVE?

Watch animals in the park with their owners – what is their relationship like?

All these are jump starts for writing – see what comes.

Animals as characters

Animals are also a great device to use in writing, especially in thrillers, mysteries and comedies. Have you ever seen a thriller and the only witness is a cat? And the cat can't talk? And you're like, WHAT HAPPENED, CAT? TELL US!

Our house got burgled once and the cat was sitting, smug, by the broken living-room window like, 'Oh, if only you saw what I saw . . .' It was so frustrating.

Could you write a scene, either made up or from real experience, from the viewpoint of an animal? How would their version of events go?

The black dog

You might have heard of depression described as a 'black dog'. It was Winston Churchill who animalised this humungous, intangible feeling and put it in a four-legged furry canine with a wagging tail and a beating heart. The black dog. Essentially Churchill made a visual, accessible way of saying 'depression is with me at the moment' and 'Where I go, it's going too.' What a great shorthand to tell friends and family that you're struggling; what an un-scary illustration of depression, a small way of finding some agency and control when lost in the thickness of mental illness. It also removes the person from the feeling by saying, 'these feelings are not me but the dog.' Which can help to lift shame and guilt.

And for me that 'black dog', like any dog, needs love, care and attention. It's another form of self-compassion. It reminds us to be kind to ourselves.

Have you ever considered giving a feeling or emotion you experience a name or identity? Is it an animal that needs taking care of?

Try writing about it.

Your own animal

Maybe you could create a new animal to describe something you might be going through. It could be a fantastical creature or beast. What are the creatures' qualities, traits and charms? Describe its teeth. Tongue. Eyes. Skin. Can you draw it?

Nine

HOW TO DEAL WITH YOUR INNER CRITIC

Everybody has one.

As if we were going to get through an entire book on creative writing without mentioning the dreaded inner critic. I think it's about time we addressed this unhelpful voice head-on rather than pretend it doesn't exist. 'Yes, I'm talking to you, INNER CRITIC. Even though I said you weren't invited, here you are. So, hey, pull up a chair . . .'

We all have an inner critic. And it seems to burst to life not only in our writing but when we are doing anything remotely out of our comfort zone or courageous, exciting, powerful or important. I have an inner critic. IRONICALLY I even had my inner critic try to chat to me when I was writing this very bit. Here are some FAQs regarding that chatty little worm.

How to tell the inner critic to shut up

Shut up.

How to really tell the inner critic to shut up

It's kind of impossible to tell our inner critic to shut up, and why would we want to? We sort of need that voice . . . not just in writing but maybe in life too . . . I'll explain.

We all have 'voices' that say we 'can't'. That tell us we're not 'good enough'. Maybe a bully voice. We have scared voices too, anxious ones that catastrophise and say, 'But what if?' My inner critic, like most people's, maybe even yours, can be loud and negative, sometimes hurtful and upsetting. In fact, nobody can be meaner to me than me, because I know all my weaknesses, trigger points and deepest fears. This internal 'voice' might pop up out of nowhere for no reason. It could be because I'm tired or emotional or stressed or hormonal. But also, I could just be bored or daydreaming. It comes up when something matters to me, when I care. Here are some things my inner voice might say: You're annoying. You're stupid. Everyone hates you. You're the worst writer in the world. Don't go to that party. You'll embarrass yourself; they've only invited you to be nice. Nobody likes you . . . etc. I could go on.

Writing down what the voice says actually helps me. It enables me to see the words for what they are: just words (and we all know how much I love words). It enables me to break the thoughts down, identify them and then challenge them. I might say, No, not everyone hates me, thank you. My sister thinks I'm the coolest girl ever, so bye. And I write down my answers too! This is important.

The more you do that, you might find you have to write them down less. You'll become 'used' to it; the critical words lose their power. You've taken ownership over your inner critic. But if you find doing this upsets you and you don't like that feeling, then please don't do it.

Intrusive thoughts don't just appear when it comes to writing. When I was a teenager I went through this horrendously annoying and uncomfortable phase of 'daring' myself. These little behavioural tendencies and compulsions were tics that would haunt and bully me all day to the point that even the simplest everyday task like boiling the kettle, crossing the road, drinking a glass of water, or waiting for a bus became a challenge on which my life depended:

If you don't make it down the stairs before the toilet stops flushing, then a monster will get you!

Who the monster was, I never found out.

If you don't finish brushing your teeth before the advert on TV finishes, you'll fail your exams!

Who knew teeth brushing was so powerful?

These small superstitions would play out. I couldn't walk over three drains, couldn't walk under signposts, and had to touch the wood on my banister every day or something bad would happen. But they added up and got me down. My brain felt like it was on a loop. Then I would beat myself up. What's wrong with you? You're so weird. Why can't you stop doing this? Your head is broken. You're going to have this for the rest of your life. This is all your fault.

It took a long time before I got the courage to talk about it. And when I did I was relieved. So many of my friends were like, 'Me too!' We found it funny to think that all day we were running around on these secret invisible, impossible self-created missions. Instantly the shame and fear removed the sting, and eventually the 'dares' went away all by themselves, along with lots of the other stuff – greasy hair, spots and angsty poetry (kind of).

But looking back, I recognise this was anxiety. A need for 'control'. At the time my parents were breaking up, I was stressed at school, I was a boiling-hot mess! It's no surprise that these 'dares' came back in abundance after my illness. Recognising these little flare-ups is so important and now I see them as 'red flags'; warning signs that I need to back off and slow down.

Peace of mind

Instead of shrinking from that anxious 'voice', I listened closely. I researched the voice. I read about it. I talked about it. I've learned to understand that even though these intrusive thoughts can be unhelpful, unwanted and uncomfortable, **they are normal**. The trick is to acknowledge them, name them if you can, and most importantly see them for what they are – a thought – and move past it. (I know this is easier said than done but with practice it does eventually click.)

Learning CBT really helped me not only understand these thoughts but also to find tools to cope (which actually work), and they can be applied to any scenario. I really recommend CBT to anybody who has found intrusive thoughts to be overwhelming. You can do a course, but I taught myself through books with support from friends and family. And then I brushed up on my skills with a CBT professional.

I want you to know this has been a great learning curve for me too. I am learning all the time. I have written 'make believe' my entire life, fuelled by my imagination, living inside a dream world. I would totally rely on my imagination like a magic door to leap out of any scenario or rocket off to some other place if something got difficult, ejecting myself out of reality.

As rosy-cosy as this pointless superpower was, essentially it was 'avoidance'. I was using my imagination to avoid the difficult things I was going through.

After my illness I found my imagination and storytelling not that useful or helpful – it felt like my imagination was what had led me to having poor mental health and becoming unwell. My negative thoughts had bluffed me so badly, I didn't feel like I could trust my own brain any more. Instead, I was running away, pretending I was OK or telling myself scary stories of why I got unwell and how I'd never recover, and that it was all my fault, blah blah blah. When, really, I had zero proof or evidence to back this up. I was scared of looking vulnerable, of appearing weak, of getting something wrong.

So I had to do the learning. Well, relearning, actually. I had to get rational, realistic and almost a bit 'science-y' in order to think clearly and see my illness for what it was: an illness. That it wasn't my fault and that it was something I could recover from. I'm telling you this because I want you to know that if the most fairy-tale, bubbleland, rose-tinted glasses wearers (me) can get their confused head around this stuff, then you can too.

That doesn't mean you can't be both a scientist and a romantic daydreaming artist, though. There is space for both.

ME 4 ME 4EVA

So it isn't Me vs Me. It's Me 4 Me 4EVA. Now I make sure in difficult moments, instead of beating myself up or giving myself a hard time, I do the opposite. I take it easy. I do something nice. It means I need more love than ever because this inner critic is really just fear. Fear is necessary. It's our body and brain's way of protecting us, guarding us and keeping us safe. Yes, it's often extremely inconvenient and very badly timed, but **it means we value ourselves**. If anything, that inner critic is there to keep us safe. That 'what if' voice is what makes our species so intelligent – it's how we prepare for danger and plan for the future. It's survival (even if it feels like it's KILLING us at the time). And when that voice rears its head when it comes to writing and releasing work into the world, it's because we care – we want others to appreciate and like what we do; we are acknowledging that we're doing something courageous and bold by putting ourselves on the line and we're nervous of failure, of being judged. And that's completely healthy and understandable; **it means we take pride in what we do**.

So, to remedy that, I try not to say 'SHUT UP!'. Instead, **I treat it like a child.** I hold my inner critic close and say, 'I know you're scared. I know you're just telling me this to protect me, to put me off writing this, sharing this, sending this out into the world, in case something unwanted comes up – like a bad thought or memory – or I don't get the reaction I'd like. Thank you for warning me.'

OR: 'I know it's easier for me not to put this out into the world. You're scared that I'll feel exposed, like I'm psychologically and emotionally running down the streets naked again. Thank you for worrying about me and not wanting me to embarass myself. I appreciate it but I'm fine.'

Sometimes I put a hand on my chest, hold myself close, rub my hands together or talk to a friend. I ask myself, 'What's the worst that can happen by putting pen to paper or setting my work free?'

Of course, sometimes those voices can be overpowering, and if you find they're overwhelming and preventing you from being the most effective person you can be or stopping you from living your best life, make sure you talk to somebody about them.

Here are some more little take-aways that might help.

Naming the inner critic

Some people name their inner critic. I know the author and activist Bryony Gordon does this. I found naming my inner critic gave 'the voice' too much power and agency, but maybe it would work for you.

It can be anything from a pet name to a celebrity's name, even something that makes you laugh.

Characterising the inner critic into a person might hand you back some control, rather than feeling this negative voice booming at you from the shadows. If you turn the critic into someone you like or admire, you might feel an affection towards them, which will dial down the fear.

Words and pictures

Thoughts are very powerful but try not to let them bluff you. **A thought is just a word and a picture**, like a story. That is all.

Thoughts are not facts that you have to buy into and believe in. Thoughts are not facts.

Try not to fight it

Try not to focus on making the negative inner critic go away or disappear; resisting will only stir and aggravate yourself – you might think it's your fault that you can't make the voice disappear or blame yourself for having such a hard time or be upset because you feel like you can't control it.

The very word 'fight' ignites our adrenaline, which is the opposite of relaxation; it creates tension, only making us more panicked and stressed. So instead (and this IS something I had to practise and still do) try floating.

Floating

'Floating' is a technique created by Dr Claire Weekes (I can't take the credit) and was a huge help for me in learning to live alongside the intrusive thoughts caused by my illness. In Weekes's book *Self-Help for Your Nerves* she speaks about not fighting unwanted thoughts and feelings but instead letting them float past us. Weekes asks why we even feel the need to do something about the thoughts at all. She encourages practising allowing unwanted thoughts and feelings to float past us; to pay them no attention. Acknowledge them if it's helpful, but try not to engage.

The book is a very short, accessible read and simply sits with you. There are no tasks or fussy bits; it isn't an exercise in itself, more a shorthand to usher your thoughts back to the present. The same principle can be applied to feelings and emotions. By simply allowing feelings and thoughts to float past us means they can begin to lose their power and actually come less and less often. If we aren't disturbed by them, they don't bother us.

'Floating' can also be used for everything. Action too! When I was unwell and couldn't eat, instead of hammering my brain with EAT! EAT! EAT! I'd float towards the fork and float food to my mouth. When I couldn't sleep, instead of blaming myself or getting frustrated, tossing and turning in bed, desperate for sleep to come, I'd float myself to rest and eventually I'd float to sleep. When I was too afraid to go to the shops, I'd float myself out of the front door. I'd float around the park. Float to have coffee with a friend. Float my book to my publisher. I ended up having 'FLOAT' written all over my house in giant hot-pink Post-it notes! This approach isn't about avoiding what's important but saying that we can do things bit by bit, without forcing ourselves into pressurised situations.

You could even try to let negative feelings you have about yourself or others float away. You can even put this technique into practice with bigger feelings. Once again, we aren't discounting or not allowing these important feelings, but we're finding another way to manage them. You could try floating through overwhelming feelings or anxieties. Floating past people who maybe aren't the best for you, past situations you could do without, past upsetting memories, words or things that hurt. Try floating past nightmares, past worries and misunderstandings. You could try floating through exams, challenges, performances. And for good stuff too – float towards someone you think is cute. Say hi.

So many of my friends have the FLOAT mantra saved as their screen savers and say it works for them too!

If you are a lover of words, as I imagine you are, if you believe in the power of them, this technique will work terrifically for you.

The same applies to writing. If you want to get stuff down but something is stopping you, perhaps you're frightened about what will come out or of it triggering something (as I was). Try not to put too much pressure on yourself, make no demands, and simply float the pen to your hand, float your pen to your page in your own time and see what comes.

You could even try calling writing floating.

I got lots of floating done today; it was great.

Maybe I'll say I'm a floater now instead of a writer?

What does the word 'float' bring up for you?

And what if?

To challenge the unhelpful 'what if?' voice, I ask myself 'what is?' and that usually gets me back on track. What if, what if, what if . . . ? Yes, but what IS? Is everything OK now, as in right now? The answer is usually yes. This is simply saying, try not to think about the future too much and stick to the now. I understand this is easier said than done, but with practice it helps.

Ten

HOW TO TAKE CARE OF A WRITER

We all need taking care of, but especially writers because, well, we're special, of course. HA!

Looking after our minds, body and creativity all come under the umbrella of self-care. This is both on and off the page. I am still trying to find my balance. To create my boundaries. To know when it's time to pause. To stand back. And writing is a great way to listen in, to gauge how you're feeling inside.

It's easy to burn ourselves out. But it isn't always easy to spot. If burnout is on the horizon, here are the signs I look for:

I'm tired even when I've slept.

I find it difficult to sleep even if I'm tired.

I'm constantly hungry.

I'm irritable.

I find it harder to concentrate than usual.

The tiniest extra task on my list is enough to send me over the edge.

I become irritable with my loved ones.

My moods swing.

I am forgetful.

I feel flat.

I make mistakes in my work, like missing out words or sentences.

My writing becomes lazy.

See how my writing can show me if I'm exhausted? I also notice that I experience a lot of these symptoms if I don't write. Writing is my meditation, my exercise, my reboot, so I find I am generally happier if I find the time to check in. What are your warning signs of burnout?

Ways to feel better

Here are some ideas on how to take care of yourself . . .

Take a breath

Whenever I do controlled breathing I feel like I'm going to hyperventilate. For me, breathing is something I just want to do without thinking about it. It's like when I go down a staircase – if I think too much about what I'm doing, I feel like I'm about to fall down them! It's really easy to forget to breathe properly when you're caught up in the flow of work. Here is a nice quick breathing technique that I love. It's so unintrusive and gentle. I actually picked it up from my son's nursery teacher.

> Simply hold your hand out in front of you with your fingers spread and, using a finger from your other hand, draw round the outline of your fingertips, as if you are drawing round your hand with a pencil. As your finger climbs up, take a deep breath in, then, as it comes down the other side of the finger, breathe out. Repeat until you feel reset.

Don't forget to eat

When you're writing, please eat. Also, in general, PLEASE EAT. You might not think you're using much energy, but writing really relies on it. If you feel you write better on an empty stomach, great, but reward yourself with food afterwards!

I always eat when writing – I am eating as I write this. I am! I'm eating little spicy rice cracker things. When I am using my brain and working hard, especially on subjects that are tricky, I get seriously hungry – and that hunger turns into HANGER pretty rapidly if I'm not careful. If my stomach is empty, it can make me anxious, and that anxiety can be hard to settle down once it's in my system and my nerves are all twisted up.

So, nuts, fruit, toast and biscuits – obvs – to keep you going, and PLENTY of hot drinks and water is an absolute MUST! I get it, sometimes we're so into what we're writing that we forget, or maybe we think we're doing nothing by sitting on our bums all day long writing – well, let me remind you, you are using a ginormous amount of power. I am at my very best when I eat three balanced meals a day and don't skip meals.

Water

While we're here, PLEASE KEEP HYDRATED. I drink over a gallon of water every day – I'm not even joking and I need it (yes, I wee a lot). I get really hot and flustered when I'm working hard. I'm using my brain and my body and my emotions all at once, and sitting in front of a screen all day can make me irritable and cranky. SO DRINK!

Keeping hydrated will also automatically improve your energy and ability to focus, all of which will make you feel better, especially if you're writing tough stuff – replenish those tears!

Hand massage

A really nice thing to do, especially if you're writing something tough, is quite simply to stop and give your hands some TLC. These hands are your instruments, so treat them well. If you were a racing-car driver, wouldn't you wash and polish your car, give it an MOT and a service? Well, your hands are your racing car and your brain is the engine, so that's what we're doing here. Hands hold a lot of nerves and tension, and they will benefit from a little squeeze from time to time. You don't need any fancy tools, just simply hand on hand. If you don't have hand cream, then coconut oil or even a little bit of olive oil would be lovely. It's also a chance to step away from your work and to practise some self-compassion!

Warming up yourself

This is a quick little trick I do when writing, especially the tricky bits. I stop. Pause. And momentarily get into the present by taking my hands and pressing them together. I hold my hands nice and tight and rub them, fast, to create warmth – like making a fire with the natural friction of my hands moving together. Within seconds my palms become toasty. This is to remind myself that I have a fire within me and that I can create energy and warmth, alone, at any moment. It might sound silly but this makes me feel less alone (and, let's face it, there isn't really an activity more solitary than writing!). I then press my warmed hands somewhere I feel needs a bit of attention and affection that day. It might be my eyes, my weary tired head or my stomach, but usually I place my hands on my chest. **Right over my heart.** It's a touchstone, a way to return to the present, to gain focus, for security, to get back into your body or an anchor if you feel you are drifting away too far. I also do this in the night when I can't sleep!

When I run workshops and ask adults to do this, at first they all look at me awkwardly, but as the sessions go on I see them coming back to this simple and effective little energiser. When I do this exercise with children in schools, they have no problem rubbing their hands together and are amazed to see how warm they can quickly make their own hands become! Let's not forget the little child inside us. Let's not grow tired of being surprised.

Feel, feel, feel

When I write, I feel. If you are not feeling it when you're writing it, how can you expect a reader to? Even if your piece is fictional, there's no reason why a high adrenaline scene shouldn't get your blood pumping and your heart beating. I always find I write quick and hard if I'm writing something tense or panicky.

There's a kind of pretentious idea that if your own work makes you cry it means you've got a massive ego – but I don't believe this at all. In the same way that it can be moving for an actor to cry on stage or a singer to cry when performing – it's not because 'I'm so good it makes me cry', it's because they are feeling it. If you are locating deep memories or hitting a source of pain, there might be tears. And if you've invested a lot into a character and something tragic happens to them, I reckon you'll feel it.

Thoughts are powerful things. So, yes, you might feel battered and bruised and exhausted and confused and emotional, but YOU did that. By writing, YOU are doing something powerful for YOURSELF and YOUR mental health. You could have done anything with your time. Look at what you're doing, where you are!

Afterwards . . .

Offloading can be exhausting and draining. Sometimes after writing I honestly feel like death warmed up, like I've been found at the bottom of a mountain with a cactus up my bum or like a zombie. But if I've given my all – what do I expect? It can make me emotional, irritable and angry. It can make me overthink, dwell and be impatient. Writing for me LONG-TERM is amazing but in the short term I'll be honest and say I'm not always the friendliest person to be around. I make sure I tell my friends and family that I'm working on something and so I'm most likely going to be a bit of a twit for the next few hours. That way I don't feel guilty. I make up for it afterwards when I've got my energy back! After an intense writing session, the best place for me is the sofa.

I put something easy on the TV that requires minimal concentration, like a cooking show or a sitcom. Nothing that is going to excite my brain and get me thinking of a trillion ideas. This is 'cooling down' for me.

I drink TONS of water and tea and eat something tasty and healthy.

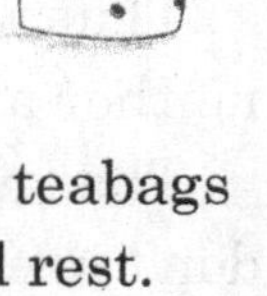

I don't talk for a bit. I don't look at my phone. I just lie down.

That is my only job.

So slam two cucumbers or cold camomile teabags over your eyeballs and have a well-deserved rest.

Being kind to yourself – really, actually kind

When we hear the phrase 'be kind to yourself' we often have no idea what that truly even means. This is what self-compassion means to me:

It means rest.

It means taking breaks.

It means forgiving myself.

It means giving myself heaps of time and patience.

It means not putting myself last.

It means not saying sorry, sorry, sorry all the time. (Here's a tip: try replacing sorry with thank you, i.e., instead of 'sorry I am late' try 'thank you for waiting for me'.)

It means not taking on too much, overfilling my diary or overcommitting (work, responsibility, even social stuff).

It means remembering I'm only responsible for my portion of the pie (i.e. not apologising for others' behaviour or feeling bad if a restaurant I've chosen for a friend isn't tasty – I didn't cook the bloody food!).

It means not beating myself up for anything.

It means remembering I am human. That I will make mistakes. And that that's OK.

That writing, like life, is not always perfect. And neither am I.

That not everyone has to do right by me. And I don't need to take it personally.

It means remembering that if someone doesn't reply to my text immediately that it doesn't mean they hate me.

It means not expecting too much from myself. Or others.

It means treating myself like little me, holding myself closely, tightly, not punishing myself.

It means doing what is within my means and within my control, giving myself limits so I have the best possible chance at whatever I'm doing that day – sleep, rest, hydrate, exercise and eat.

It means knowing it's not all in my control.

It means being OK with uncomfortable feelings.

It means keeping on top of my negative automatic thoughts and my CBT. And accepting myself . . .

This is just the surface. You can learn more about true self-compassion and I really advise it – it has improved my mental health and writing so much.

In what ways could you be kinder to yourself? Write them down.

It might seem silly. It might seem luxurious and hugely privileged. But it's not. It's important.

Make yourself comfy

Writing hurts. No, it actually hurts. My fingers cramp, my wrists strain and my back – ouch – no, my shoulders, OH NO, no, don't go there, two actual cement bollards. It's like I need a twenty-four-hour massage – but at the same time DON'T YOU DARE TOUCH ME!

My ribs hurt, my chest hurts, my eyes feel like they are bleeding. I need a million wees, I'm so thirsty, my neck makes all these strange noises – it crunches. My neck CRUNCHES.

Don't suffer – pimp up your writing space and make yourself as comfy as you possibly can. Cushions, blankets, PJs, slippers. I often go to bed stinking of Deep Heat and arnica.

I try to take care of my core to support my back (but sit-ups are hard work), I try to stretch and take breaks – but I probably don't do enough. Check in with your body and mind. Take care of that racing car.

And remember that your space, no matter how small or public, is sacred. Be proud of it, treat it with respect. It doesn't have to be clean and tidy but do make it cosy and safe, make it yours. Some people like to keep their plots, plans and character profiles on the walls; others like their writing environments to be neutral, a blank slate. Personally, my work in progress is very private to me – I don't want anybody else looking at my notes! But see what works for you. Plants, lights, ornaments, images of things that make you happy. Photographs of loved ones to keep you company, books and inspiration close by.

Being hard on yourself

You might have good writing stints and not-so-good writing stints – days when you could write for ever and the flow is just gorgeous, and days when you just can. not. The work just isn't coming. Blood from a stone. Don't be hard on yourself. Just take yourself away and do something else. Have a lie-down, have a walk, see a friend, watch a movie, treat yourself . . .

Definitely do treat yourself

I have writer friends who gift themselves when they've achieved word counts or to celebrate deadlines and publications. I heard that Queen Jacqueline Wilson buys herself a new ring to acknowledge the release of every book she writes (and she has a LOT of books and a lot of rings). Treating yourself is a really lovely way of thanking your body and brain for its hard work. I mean, writing is just about the loneliest, zero-colleague job/hobby you can get. Nobody else is going to buy you a coffee and a slice of chocolate cake from the cafe! So, just as important as buying yourself a little gift to say 'well done' to yourself, treat your body too. A face mask. A book. A game. A pot of nail polish. A ticket to a show, gig or football match. In the meantime you could set yourself mini goals – if I do 500 words, I'll have a cup of hot chocolate; when I reach 1,000 words, I'll have a bath . . .etc.

Writing is already challenging enough; we don't need to make the job any harder. Drink, snack, sleep, move, open the windows; make sure the environment is as lux as possible with everything you need to get the words down.

Oh, and please wee.

Can you believe that up until only recently I would hold back on weeing until I had reached a word count? Not as self-torture, just to keep me at my desk (which, hold on, definitely counts as self-torture!). I mean, I used to see weeing as a TREAT. A TREAT. HUH? You know you're a hard-working martyr when you relieve your bladder as a REWARD. So now, I am pleased to say, I wee when I need to.

A room for a writer

I find it really hard writing in cafes. I get panicked about the plug socket, wondering if my laptop will run out of battery, if the cafe owner will get annoyed at me for being there for four hours and only buying one cup of tea and a brownie, and what if someone steals my bag? What if someone peers over my shoulder and laughs at my silly little words? What if I see someone I know and have to talk? Anyway, there is NO WAY any cafe has enough toilet paper for all my wees. For me, cafes are too distracting to work in. I like to people-watch too much. Let's be real – I like to cake-watch too much too. Yet I find working in libraries too quiet sometimes. So finding a room to write in is really precious.

I grew up in a squashed-up lovely little flat in Brixton, South London. There were five of us: Mum, Dad and my two siblings – both of whom were hyperactive, annoying and LOUD (as was I). It was a lovely home and I have very many happy memories of it. To me we all had enough room, but it was a case of learning to find a breathing space, a moment, in the corner of a room. My mum had set up an area in the living room to work where she would click away as we swung each other round in circles behind her with the TV volume turned up to a million, fought over toys, screamed and shouted and very BADLY hooted on the recorder, used the furniture like an adventure playground and the floor was always lava or shark-infested water, wrestled on the floor, pretended to host our own cooking shows and then performed the Spice Girls. Somehow she got work done.

My dad transformed a hallway airing cupboard into a standing desk where he managed his business. I would write from the top bunk in my shared bedroom before bed, my orange lava lamp spilling its light, scribbling on sheets of paper using a massive hardback textbook as a desk.

Well, I've been writing professionally full-time for over fifteen years now and I only JUST got my first ever proper desk. I've written on makeshift tables made from planks of wood and bricks, an old desk with a wobbly leg that kept dropping on my thigh with an eye-watering smack, a deconstructed rusty sewing-machine table, my lap, a breakfast tray (like what you'd eat your dinner from if you were in a hospital bed), the arms of sofas and many kitchen tables and back to writing from bed again using my knobbly knees as a writing surface! I wrote on shiny receipt paper during my time working on a shop floor, where the biro glides around like an ice skater and I had to write in little neat columns, with stories in strips like Father Christmas's naughty list. I wrote, for a while, standing up, by hand on an easel, which was strange. Put it this way: if there was paper up for grabs, I was gonna write on it. If there was a hard surface up for grabs, I was gonna write on it. For a bit I went to work with MY MUM (like a child does in the summer holidays) to borrow a desk space. I also used the desk at the hairdresser's I worked at, wisps of cut hair and blobs of hair dye and coffee rings marking my paper (which I stole from the printer). In the acknowledgements in the backs of my books are thank-yous to all the people I borrowed from over the years. Without them I don't think my stories would have been possible.

I, maybe like you, still dream of a writer's shed. I know writers who do have them. This higgledy-piggledy lovely pathway from their house, through their garden, overgrown with wilderness and submerged in birdsong, leading to this romantic Narnia-style grotto hidden under some willow tree. A hut completely dedicated to dreaming and make-believe . . . But sometimes you've just got to make do with what you have. Your writer's room can be inside your head. If you practise enough, you can make space. There can be a pocket inside your mind completely committed to you and your writing, creating and dreaming. And the more you travel there, the quicker you'll know the route. The quicker you'll be able to transport and escape, the more work you'll get down, the more you'll be able to squeeze in around life and your responsibilities. You can grow and sprawl, finding your way like a flower does through a crack in the pavement. Through all the chaos and loudness. It is important to have space for yourself to think and write. For many of us it is a luxury and a privilege. (Some people have access to these spaces and never even use them if you can imagine?!) If you can find a nook, a corner, a quiet spot of some kind, then that's all you need. A small room is all you need for big ideas.

NOW BLAST OFFFFFFFF . . .

Social media

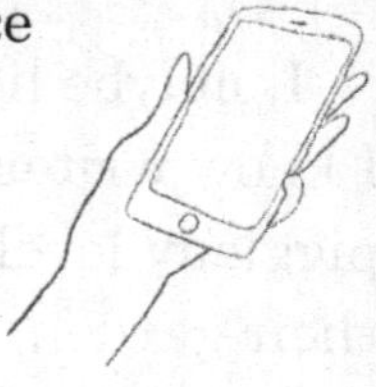

It can be a great place to show your face as a writer. I know many writers who have strong social media platforms who get the chance to shake their tailfeathers by writing well in their captions and descriptions. Social media, when used effectively and healthily, at its best can be a brilliant way of showing your talent – there you can write from the heart informally and use humour to speak to your readers. You can write powerfully and be direct and there is something remarkably raw and unfiltered that I love about it.

Social media also allows you to connect with other writers and artists, and in the lonely world of writing that can be an absolute lifeline. Other writers are like colleagues in the open-plan office of our minds. Just knowing there are thousands of others tapping away, pouring out their hearts, boiling the kettle and doing a million wees makes me feel so comforted. Social media can be very inspiring, particularly when I'm on a writing stint or in the thick mist of a deadline. I like hopping on and seeing these little windows of life, bursts of conversation, almost like a busy train or faces in a cafe. They can build community.

And when talking about my illness, I can honestly say I felt so supported and held by my friends on social media. It's been an incredibly powerful shorthand for me to speak to others who have or are going through similar challenges. I like the way it allows me to connect with others but still be in the safety, privacy and comfort of my home.

That said, it might not help to see people 'living their best life' if you, quite frankly, aren't.

Remember, sometimes life on social media is edited. It has been designed by the user, who gets to be the architect of their dreams; filtered, scripted, rehearsed, edited, etc. And so much of this 'living your best life' is not even a real life. I find it hard to follow writers telling the world how wonderfully well their books have sold, that their work's being turned into a movie, that they've been commissioned to write this, that they've won an award. I find it hard to get the energy to keep writing and make more stories, to not take it personally. I find it easy to feel inadequate and to give myself a bad time. And all those insecurities ramp up once again, which tell me I'm not good enough, cool enough, clever enough, funny enough.

So what do I do? I step away from it and I remind myself that everyone is simply doing their best. That's it. That nobody is intentionally setting out to harm anyone or make anybody feel bad (unless they are a troll – but that's another story). That most people will probably feel the same way I do. That maybe there'll even be people out there triggered by my account. So I have to consider that too. Instead, I plant myself in reality. I hold tight to what I have. The real things: my home, my partner, my son. My family that I eat with and argue with as humans do. My friends who I actually see for coffee and walks by the river. I hold tight to the wonderful heavy casserole pot that makes all the best sauces. My bright pink lipstick. My orange tree. My books and, of course, my writing.

What do you hold on to?

Write about it . . .

The guilty feeling

I always have that feeling that I'm not working hard enough, quick enough. That there aren't enough hours in the day. Because of that annoying voice in my head that loves to tell me that I'm not smart enough, clever enough, academic enough, legit enough. That I'm a fraud. I feel I have to work extra hard to make up for that. Now I am a mum too I feel my seconds transforming into hours into days into weeks into months where I still haven't written that thing I promised myself I was going to. Go with the way of life and don't beat yourself up.

Living is writing.

Impulse, instinct and gut reaction

Trust your words. Trust your gut feeling. Believe in your story and the way you're telling it. Believe that you are the person to tell this story and prove it by the way you write. Writing is more than just communication. It's magic – and if you don't believe in it, how can you ask a reader to?

How to tell writer's block to move out of your way

Get out of the way.

(Writer's block doesn't exist.)

Why I don't believe in writer's block

If you are writing something and enjoying it, you will not get stuck. If you are writing for yourself from the right place, the words and the story will burst out of you and you will find a flow. It will be like bursting a water main. Try to write for yourself because you are enjoying it; don't force yourself. If you have a story to tell, a character that is haunting you like a ghost to be written, trust me, you will know about it.

Ways to get past writer's block (if you insist)

Save your work and leave it where it is.

If it's on a desktop, hide it; if it's on paper, put it in a drawer out of sight – for at LEAST a week!

Or maybe it's time to share it? (More on that later.)

Get inspired! Need more brain food? Go and see a film, go for a walk, see a play, meet a friend, go to a gallery, read, read, read, read, read or listen to music.

If you are stuck on a project but still want to write, move on to a different project. I always have more than one project on my slate purely for this reason. They all move at different paces; they all use different parts of my brain and they inspire and feed each other!

Try some of the exercises in this book to refresh your head and unblock.

LIVE! Do some living! You can't write if you don't live.

Take a break.

Get some sleep.

Exercise. Some of my best ideas happen when I'm exercising – it uses a different part of the brain and gets the blood thumping.

Do something practical. I love cooking – I find it relaxing and it always clears my head.

I've said it before but it's worth saying again: get outdoors. We can learn so much from nature just by being around it. We have a constant source of inspiration right on our doorsteps.

Change your writing space. I just changed mine from a quiet dark room overlooking other houses (which I thought would be better for inspiration – it wasn't; it just made me look like a stalker or like I was in *Rear Window*) to facing out towards the world where, although it's more noisy, it's much brighter and I can see trees and people. I feel more connected to the world.

Switch it up

Here are some practical things you can do to mix up your writing rhythms:

Listen to a radio station you'd never normally listen to.

Sleep at the other end of the bed so that waking up feels different.

Pick up something from the supermarket that you wouldn't normally.

Borrow a book from the library that you wouldn't normally choose.

Call up, or go for a walk with, an old friend or relative who you haven't spoken to for a really long time. Ask them, how are you? What have you been up to?

Run outside. Take a different route. By the river, through the park. Look up, look down there and round there. Set your alarm clock an hour earlier and get outdoors when the day is just beginning. If you run a lot, try walking this time, go at a slower pace today, soak it all up! Come back, write about it.

Take yourself to a show, something you wouldn't normally watch.

Watch a film/show/documentary that Netflix does NOT recommend to you.

Take recommendations for books, films and shows from friends and family and follow them through.

Walk a different way to the shops. Buy something new. Write about it.

Or come up with your own ideas. None of these are prescriptions; you don't even have to write about them. They're just suggestions: healthy ways to break up a certain headspace or state of mind, to distract, to give your work a breather, to do something different, to give your creativity a fresh spin.

Potato-wedge it

My dad loves London pubs. He believes much literary history lives inside a London pub. That in the fabric of the seats, the stains on the tables, the stickiness in the patterned carpets you'll find echoes of the greats. If you listen close enough, you'll hear the ghostly whispers of horror stories, love stories, mystery, poetry and memoir. Anyway, he used to occasionally drink in a pub that did the best potato wedges (this story is gross by the way) and we'd sometimes go as a real treat. The wedges would come, fat, perfectly beige and boiling hot, served with four little pots: tomato sauce, mayonnaise, ground pepper and salt.

He'd drink his pint and I'd sit with my chips.

I'd dip the ends of a wedge into ketchup and salt at one end, mayo and pepper at the other, then switch it up, finding the best combination until I'd exhausted all my greedy options and my mouth was confused, I needed water and a lie-down. I'd find the last few wedges tasted best on their own as they were. Untouched. Natural. Pure.

What I'm saying is this: find balance in your writing by experimenting. Go from one extreme to the other. Be abstract, be surreal, be romantic, be over-the-top dramatic, be cheesy, corny, comical, minimal, restrained, pretentious, snobby, chaotic, subtle. Write 'badly'. Be saccharine. Emotional. Manipulative. Say it all, give it all, give nothing.

Try it all and you will get there.

Eleven

HIDDEN NOTES FROM THE WRITER'S BIBLE

There isn't one. I made that up, sorry.

Some myth-busters about the writer species

~~To be a writer you have to be old~~

You can be any age to write. I've taught writing workshops to nursery children! One of my publishers says that 'books are vitamins for the brain'. It is never too early to read, write and tell stories. But it is also never too late to begin.

~~To be a real writer you have to be dead~~

All the writers we studied at school were dead white men. How was this inspiring to me and my classmates made up of young South-London girls? To make the ambition of being a writer a reality, the power has to be handed to the writer and shown that it is POSSIBLE.

It is possible. Voices from everybody, everywhere. We want alive voices, young voices, with stuff to say. Voices like yours!

~~To be a writer you have to be really clever and academic~~

I never thought I'd become a published author. I thought I had more chance of landing on the moon, and yet here I am. I studied creative writing at university, but truthfully (sorry to be so honest) I think I'd have got more experience continuing to work at the hairdresser's where I was a part-time scrubber and sweeper, because the hair salon is such a home for real-life stories and vulnerability and activity. And I wouldn't be in debt. Livid.

~~To be a writer you have to have read all the classics~~

Well, we already know that's not true. (Ahem, remember *The Count of Monte Cristo* Volume 2?)

~~To be a writer you have to use big, impressive, posh words~~

Those words mean nothing if they come from nowhere and nobody can understand them.

Write like YOU. Not how you think a writer is meant to sound.

~~Writers are really serious~~

Huh?

~~Writers are introverts~~

OK.

~~Writers are boring~~

Some are, yes, but I bet there are also boring acrobats and pop stars and scientists.

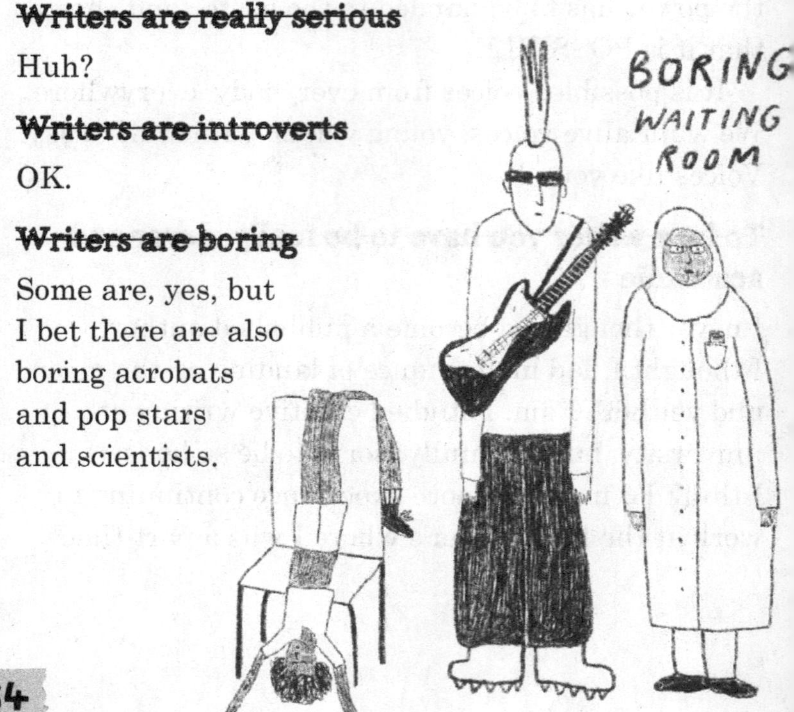

~~Writers like being alone~~

This one doesn't.

~~Writers like being in Victorian attics wearing an old scraggy nightie and writing with a quill by candlelight~~

Sounds TERRIFYING.

~~Writers are rich~~

Are they?

How to be a real writer

Write.

Twelve

EDITING AND SHARING YOUR WORK

Sharing is not the end goal of writing.

You never, ever have to share. I always make this clear at the very start of any of my workshops or masterclasses. Taking part is showing up and that is all. If I was in a workshop, I would dread being picked on to read out loud. It's part of the reason many writers are put off writing – maybe they've had a negative experience like being chosen to read out loud in school. It can be exposing, humiliating and damaging to our confidence. It is possible to be brave enough to write but not want to share. You can be an extrovert and an introvert at the same time! You also don't have to match your work. You're not twins! Just because you write gothic horror doesn't mean you have to present yourself in this way. Just because you write happy stories doesn't mean you have to be always smiling with a red clown nose on your face.

Sharing is not the end goal of writing.

That said, you might feel compelled to share. And if so – how generous! And courageous, and why not say gorgeous too? I am sure you'll feel liberated, relieved and comforted once you do. There are many ways to share your work, but here are some things to consider before you do . . .

How will it make you feel?

The first time I wrote about my illness, about six months after I had been hospitalised, was for a blog. I was not even fully recovered at this point; I was still quite unwell. On medication, in therapy and certainly not 'back to my old self' or at a place of peace. My confidence was below zero. The ground still shook when I walked. I fizzed. The writing wrote itself. It poured out of me uncontrollably; it was impulsive. I don't even remember doing it. I was still finding my sea legs. I wrote the blog entry on my phone, sent it to the blog along with some photos (which I couldn't look at without crying) and off it went.

Within twenty-four hours the post had gone viral. I was hearing from old school friends, friends of my parents, people who had cared for me when I was unwell and strangers that had shared my story. It had happened: my work had connected.

But the next morning after that, I felt terrible. I immediately regretted putting it out there and knew there was no going back. It was too exposing, too honest, too revealing. I sounded too vulnerable, too 'broken'. My brain began to spiral. Oh, that inner critic came with a vengeance. What if I would never work again after this? What if nobody took me seriously again? What if my illness defined me? What if everybody patronised me and felt sorry for me?' Of course they didn't, but I felt like everybody was watching me. I believed any kind, supportive messages were from a place of judgement or pity. It was ironic – my work was recognised, out there, but I couldn't leave the house. It felt like a sick joke.

I didn't relapse but I became very anxious again; I felt many of my negative feelings roaring back. In fact, it was the very 'outing' of my illness that made my insecurities fire off. Once I recovered, I understood the impact of that blog piece. I could read the messages of solidarity and gratitude and see them for what they were, and the writing eventually got me to a stable place of health and wellness. But it wasn't overnight and it wasn't linear.

I've been asked before why I felt the need to share. I have thought about this lots. I think it's about ownership. During recovery, many of my loved ones would say, 'That wasn't you, Laura. It was the illness.' Then I got to a place where I was like, 'No, that was me; that is me. It's all me. All of it.' That allowed me to feel proud of my recovery and protective of myself – in a postitive way.

Another reason was for awareness. Nobody had ever told me about an illness like this. I hadn't known it was possible. I had a platform as a writer and an ability to communicate, so I wanted to write the book I wish I'd read when I was unwell. I didn't want to pretend that the illness doesn't exist and just add to the conspiracy. Now I find that if

I go for stretches or long periods of time without talking or writing about my illness, I feel more anxious. Keeping it around makes me feel safe; it's pretending it never happened that worries me.

So am I glad I shared? Of course. But it's important to remember that your own mental health and wellness is TOP PRIORITY. Only share it if suits you.

My family were also very nervous and anxious about me writing about it. My illness had affected them too – but when they began to see the results, how much more like myself I felt, how I was processing, learning, healing and not talking about it all so bloody much, they couldn't argue with my decision.

Editing

Unconfident with my spelling and grammar at school, I was constantly in a losing battle with my worst enemy – THE TEACHER'S BIG RED PEN. I've learned the best and most trustworthy reliable editor is TIME. Give it time. It is so tempting to keep going back to that same file, tinkering, touching, editing. LEAVE IT.

The best bit of advice I ever got when it comes to writing a manuscript (although I rarely keep to it) is **DON'T LOOK BACK.** Keep writing and moving forward until you've written a first draft. You can edit afterwards.

The dream process would be:

Know roughly in your mind what you wish to write

Write it

Leave it

Forget about it (ha ha, as if)

Print it out (costly on the environment so try to read it on a screen if not too difficult)

Read it with fresh eyes

Go again

Of course it doesn't always work out like this. It's irresistible not to touch it and my printer never seems to work. And yet here we are.

When you've finished a piece of writing you can choose to leave the material where it is – that might be enough for you – or you can think about polishing it, making it gleam. This can be for yourself – some people find editing relaxing and fun! (I KNOW!) Or you might want to get it into shape for new eyes. There are lots of ways to do this. Most writers will edit their work themselves: this is self-editing. Here, as well as the boring stuff (spelling, grammar) you can look for areas to improve. Ask yourself questions like, have I described that hedgehog to the best of my ability? Self-editing is not about self-sabotage but about marinating, bubbling and boiling like a good one-pot feast. Maybe keep a 'dump page' open where you can add new thoughts and bits that come to you, but let the text breathe, have distance, have space, have time and get on with a new project or some good old living!

Some writers will then pass the version they are most happy with on to an editor of some kind for feedback, advice, suggestions and cuts (AND TO SPOT A LOT MORE MISTAKES!). In a professional capacity, this might be with a commissioning editor (a person who publishes books for their actual job, working with the author to refine the text), who usually works at a publisher or similar organisations. But I wouldn't recommend just giving your work over or ever paying for an edit unless they are from a trusted source. A friend or teacher could help you just as well with 'ironing out the creases' to make your material more effective. But trust yourself. In my experience, editors usually say 'less is more'. DAMMIT. Why do I always remember that towards the end of a book?

Remember that writing in its raw, pure state is very exciting to read. And beautiful too. Remember that talent, truth and heart is rare and can be spotted a mile away and that the misspelling of the odd word here or there will not make or break how your work is received. Remember: you're writing for humans who understand that we all make mistakes. Cut yourself some slack and concentrate on the words, not how tidy it is. Fight for the story, not perfection.

Feedback

I get asked to give feedback on creative writing all the time and I'd be lying if I said that doesn't overwhelm me. Not because I don't enjoy reading new work. I feel very privileged to be asked to do it. However, I am no judge. If you write something and you like it, that's all that matters. The audience always comes second. Of course, if that work was to be published, that's an entirely different matter. I'm not a commissioning editor or a publisher. I am just a storyteller – like you.

That said, if you do want to move forward and think about letting go of your work, it can be really useful to get some feedback. You might honestly have no idea what to make of it otherwise.

Every time I share my work with my partner or family, I regret it. They NEVER seem to be able to say the right thing. It's not fair on me and my work, but it also isn't fair on them because I'm putting them in a compromising position. When asking for feedback from loved ones consider that, firstly, they love you so they are probably going to love what you write. Secondly, if they don't love what you write, they are probably not going to say so because they don't want to hurt you. And, lastly, they can't really stand back and see it objectively because they know you.

Also, some other things to keep in mind . . .

They might have their own memories or trauma from the same situation.

They might not be ready to hear about it.

It might trigger or bring up painful memories for them.

I would say to find people in your life that you know who aren't too close to you, who you can trust, who read. You want an honest, balanced opinion, but remember that it is just an opinion. (Your sibling might not be able to give you a neutral, honest, genuine opinion simply because you annoyed them that day!)

Instead, to avoid conflict and compromise, build a network of people you trust and who you feel comfortable sharing writing with, and, as a return gesture, offer to read their work too. Chances are that if you're looking for feedback, there will be many others looking for healthy feedback they can trust too. There are writers' rooms, writers' blogs, workshops and clubs for this kind of stuff. These relationships can be really crucial and fruitful for you.

How to take criticism

With a massive pinch of salt. I know you know this but it can be hard to remember in the moment. Just because somebody says something about your work doesn't mean you have to change it. It's harsh, but

not everyone is going to love what you do, and why do they have to? What somebody makes of your work is actually none of your business – the same way I hate anchovies. It's not the anchovy's fault.

Remember, sometimes people give feedback because they feel they should. I know writers who deliberately leave mistakes in their work just so an editor has some changes to make so they don't dig too deeply into the rest of their work.

Trust yourself. You are writing because you felt an urge. Because you HAD to. Do YOU like it? What do YOU think? You write for you.

If you're writing for a specific age group, like picture books for young children, then it helps to read to young children – just not any who know and love you! When I first started writing I used to visit my old school to read to the students there. You'll get honest feedback from kids, trust me!

How not to upset people

This is tricky but manageable. When writing from personal experience, our stories often overlap with reality. Your story might include people from your life and perhaps not upsetting them is holding you back from telling the story. I had this when writing about my illness. I would say to let the first draft belong to you: write what you want to write (if you are able to). Let your hand and heart guide you. A first draft of anything is for the writer alone. If you want to share it, then you need to think about ways to include people from your life without upsetting anybody and dishonouring yourself.Everybody is different, but here is what I did:

I wrote my first pass for me without thinking about anybody else, their reaction, their response or even their feelings. That way I felt my story was told, I felt cleansed and free and got my memories in order. (Nobody else ever read this version.)

When I was ready, I came back to the work and edited it, taking out bits that I didn't feel comfortable about sharing.

When I was OK with that draft, I shared the work with a commissioning editor (from a trusted source) who went over everything and made suggestions and gave feedback, illuminating anything that was too exposing. This was helpful because the editor was able to see the work objectively.

Then I went over the manuscript again.

I sent that manuscript to all the people mentioned to check they were happy with the text. Some of these people came back with changes and we talked them through. If I didn't send the manuscript to them, I made sure they remained unnamed and/or I disguised their appearances.

The book then had a 'legal read' to make sure my own and others' privacy was protected. A legal read catches anything that could potentially trip you up at a later date or might reveal something you wouldn't want the world to know. It was useful in my experience to conceal professionals' names or people I had met in hospital who might not want to be so open about what they went through.

When the book was published, we printed this in the opening pages: The events described here are based on memories of my experience. The identifying features of some people and places have been changed in order to protect their privacy. Any similarities are purely coincidental. And that seemed to do the trick.

This might seem awfully far away for you but it's good to keep in mind in case such details are stopping you from writing what you want.

How to write truthfully without writing the whole truth

Of course you want to write the truth. You want to keep your story yours. It is completely possible to tell a true story and hold bits back for yourself. I find it's important to not overshare if you don't feel comfortable but, also, keep some bits for you.

Rejection

Look into any industry and there will be famous rejection stories. Bands and musicians that couldn't get record deals, who were dropped and are now legendary. Actors who were the thirty-fifth choice on a long list for a certain role and who went on to win an Oscar. Stories that have gone on to become Hollywood blockbusters that have been written by writers with enough rejection letters to wrap round the Earth twice. Stephen King's book *On Writing* is great for these types of resilient reminders (which us authors need to hear!).

My neighbour recently finished the second draft of her memoir. She sent it to me; I thought it was so moving, it blew me away. She said she found writing it so beneficial for her mental health and healing process. She asked when I thought it was OK to send to an agent; I said only she could know the answer to that. I don't know her that well and it's her story. She worked on it a little more but then she sent it off.

Several days later she got a really warm 'thanks but no thanks' letter from an agent and began jumping for joy. She even sent me a massive bag of chocolate almonds to say thank you. I was thinking, 'What the hell is going on here? The chick's just had a rejection letter and she's elated! She's running around like she's got a book deal.'

I asked her if she was OK, secretly thinking, did she read the email wrong? Is she seeing the same words I'm seeing?

She said, 'Oh, Laura, I feel so happy. This is my first rejection. I've waited my whole life for this moment. Now I feel like a real writer.'

She went on to say how liberated she felt having sent her story out into the world, that it wasn't a giant rain cloud over her head any longer. That the end goal was not being published, it was simply in the act of letting go, of pressing send and setting herself free.

A cool thing to try

I've had several pen pals over the years. Embarrassingly enough my husband was once my pen pal when we were fourteen – and look how that worked out! There are lots of ways to make a pen pal – you could begin with a friend at school (just because you see each other all the time doesn't mean you can't write letters). You could try writing to a grandparent, cousin or distant relative. Start small and see how it goes.

(I ALWAYS put balloons in my pen pal letters. They are the most lightweight, cheapest and happiest gift that keeps on giving in the world.)

Have you ever written a love letter?

Another cool thing to try

Can't find a place to show off your wicked way with words? Make one! Does your school, college or workplace have a magazine or paper? If not: create a zine. See if you can rope a tutor in to help you (any good teacher loves all this extra-curricular stuff and it will earn you brownie points too – **MAKE THE EDUCATION SYSTEM WORK FOR YOU, GUYS**, rinse the amenities the building has to offer). Try the English, art or drama departments. This is a beautiful way of bringing community together while helping you stand out as a writer and creative. If you do create a paper, congratulations (and please send me one) – it will always be something REAL, proof you can use in the future for your portfolio and CV. As well as your wonderful writing, it shows initiative and innovation. It also gives you something substantial to keep for yourself. To show friends and family and be proud of. And it's a great way to meet other writers and creatives.

You could create a podcast . . . What will it be about? How can it showcase your writing and point of view? This is something we did with my own podcast Zombie Mum! You could link up with other creativies and host a platform for the arts. Reach out to other podcasts you like listening to and see if any of their guests will feature on yours! This can be a great way to build momentum and promote across different outlets. You can return the favour by appearing on their podcast!

You could create a blog. Here you can write as much as you want about whatever you want. Take photographs or include artwork from your friends. Connect with other writers, build a network! For extra content you could run competitions or commission new work around a certain theme. Many writers starting out would be happy to do this in exchange for their work to be showcased.

Or even start a radio at your school/college/ workplace! Join forces with a budding engineer – it might be a fun project for anybody with a keen interest in production.

Another really cool idea

Live readings and open mics (a showcase of different art forms but usually music, stand-up or poetry in a variety-show format where everyone gets a chance to share work in a carousel of talent) are all

EXCELLENT ways of getting your work out there, and quick! Getting immediate feedback, reactions and responses can get you and your work noticed, improve your confidence, help you find your writing voice and even help edit your work. I got picked up by a publisher from a live reading so I really recommend them.

You could create an open mic, live reading, cafe event or poetry slam at your school or college in the evening or in your lunch break. If not, you could ask a local bookshop or community hall to help you host.

To get things rolling you could invite a well-known poet, singer, speaker to perform at your event to draw a crowd. See if your school or college would be able to support the artists visit by covering a fee and travel expenses – it's worth a shot! Most writers love to hear from enthusiastic young people and support growing ideas.

Tips for hosting live events

- Give your event a GREAT name.
- Invite a talented visual person to create eye-catching artwork for your event.
- Publicise well, invite everybody, include everyone.
- Be fair, inclusive and unbiased with running orders and scheduling.
- Ask a friend who is good at tech to help you with quality sound and lighting so everybody is heard properly (music always needs a bit more support).

- Think about the space. Nobody wants to read or share their work in a big, empty, brightly lit, echoey sports hall where the acoustics are terrible. If you have a large space, use soft cushions, rugs and furnishings to fill it. You could do a 'cabaret' style set-up with tables and chairs or have the audience sit on the floor for a more relaxed environment.
- If you can only drum up a small crowd to begin with, don't let that put you off – choose a small, intimate space and trust that your event will grow the more you do it!
- Remind all artists/performers/players/readers to stick around to watch and support all the other acts (not just your mates).
- If you're performing, bring a crowd.
- Come prepared! If you're reading from paper, have it printed out clearly so you can project your voice and make eye contact with the audience.
- Always have a little sneaky extra something up your sleeve for an encore (you never know, babes) or just in case you change your mind and want to read something else on the day. Make the most of your slot.
- Make sure people can find your work afterwards. You could signpost them to future readings, your socials or hand out homemade zines and booklets (it's what I did and doesn't have to be expensive or fancy!).

- If you want your words to be heard but you don't want to read them yourself, try asking a friend who enjoys public speaking or an actor to read for you. You could also ask a friend who can sing or play an instrument to perform your work as a song.

Anon.

You may have seen 'Anon.' at the bottom of some poems instead of a poet's name. Anon. is an abbreviation for 'anonymous'. It can sometimes mean the writer is unknown but it can also mean that the writer has chosen not to publish their name with their writing. There can be a number of reasons why someone might choose to do this. The author might not feel safe sharing their name, they might not want to hurt or upset anybody else, they might just enjoy putting out work out without claiming it as their own, they might not want praise or criticism. Maybe the writing is controversial, exposing or revealing.

Remember that you can always use 'Anon.'.

Writers' club

You could start a writers' club, with members taking turns to lead each session. You could even work your way through this book in groups. Remember, you don't have to share your creations but you could share your progress. I'm in a writers' group in which we discuss what we're working on and our progress but we never share our writing. Never underestimate the strength of a writers' club – a group I had a hand in forming at a school is still going now, some eight years later, though all the original members moved on! The group has a legacy that has outlived us. Keep in mind what I said about writing sometimes being a lonely, isolating journey – having others write/create alongside you can be comforting and supportive.

I read some graffiti on a bridge last week:

If you want to go fast, go alone. If you want to go far, go together!

Put on a show

I mean, why not? In my final year of school I asked the school secretary if I could put a play on one lunchtime. He looked at me like, 'Er . . . yeah . . ?' Like he was surprised I even had to ask. I wrote a little play, we ran auditions, my friends helped with set and costume, and school even printed out official tickets! I will never forget what it did for my self-belief. It was a great way to establish my writing, hear it on stage and let people knew I meant business! That said, I never want to read that play ever again. (CRINGE!)

Stories are the seed

Theatre, film, music, animation – they all begin with words. Like my cringey school play, writing down a short, simple story and breaking it into characters can invite a whole community to come together and make something happen. Just because.

It begins with story, always.

It's about making the most of the opportunity. If there is no stage, create one.

What could you do?

Where to go next . . .

The fairytale road to publishing is simple: you write your work, you meet an agent, they say 'we love it!', that agent takes your work to editors, one of them says 'YES PLEASE!' to publishing it and that's it – your book is published.

It's also unrealistic.

The reality of that story is very different. Every author has their own journey but there is usually a lot more heartache, disappointment, rejection and most certainly a LOT MORE NOTES along the way! Sadly, the publishing industry is overworked – as you can imagine, it takes an enormous amount of time and effort to read and make books all day long. An agent is usually the best route to reach a publisher; otherwise, more often that not, your hard work will land on the desk of an intern (someone on work experience) who will have the unfortunate job of opening submissions and sending out rejection letters! (Trust me, I've done it!) And the road stops there. **But we don't want the road to stop!** So where to go next?

I got published not by submitting my work to an agent or publisher (although I have done that too – it just didn't work! Told you!) but by learning my stories off by heart and performing the work by playing characters and telling stories at theatres, pubs, libraries, festivals, schools . . . The work made me feel safe, like I could hide behind the mask of the characters. Performance was a shortcut – it made me feel like I was being 'active' in trying to get my words heard. It meant not sitting in a lukewarm slush pile on an intern's desk awaiting the dreaded rejection letter. It was a trapdoor, another way in. Without seeing the work nobody could critique my work, judge it, touch it, catch it. I felt I could avoid scrutiny. Reading live allowed me to control how I wanted my work to be digested, to get my point across and get instant feedback too (believe me, you learn pretty quickly what a live audience likes and doesn't – it's like editing in real time). Reading at live literary events also meant I could get noticed by publishers straight away.

And it actually worked. Aged twenty-two I got published. I still don't think I'd ever have got that break if it wasn't for those early days of reading my work aloud, using all the ways of sharing I've described above – writers' clubs, open mics, slams and events – to get my work out there.

You see, there are many ways to become a writer. But the best way is really quite simple: write.

I'd always say that if the requests stopped, then I'd stop. But one reading rolled into another, one school visit into a workshop, into a commission, into a book. Sometimes it would go quiet . . . but something always came in the end and if the work didn't, the ideas did. I never quite had the confidence to ever not have a part-time job. I have always felt that being writer isn't what my dad would call a 'proper job'. Teachers at school didn't really take my ambition very seriously, so neither did I. It was clowning around. It was too much fun to be considered work and it came too easily to be a career. Being paid for it would be too much to ask. I had to learn that having an agent represent you (even a great one), being published (yes, even by the greatest publishers) and having books in brilliant shops on high streets, even being in windows, does not overnight a successful author make.

It takes time, rejection, practice, effort, slog, long hours with a sore back in your pyjamas eating mattresses of toast and 40,000 cups of tea. But when it works . . . when you realise in your hand is not a pen but a wand – that is when the real magic comes.

And, oh boy, is it magic, and just like that, suddenly . . .

you are a story.

Resources

Asking for help is the best thing I ever did. If you feel you need any support with difficult issues or themes raised in this book, do talk to a trusted adult, or reach out to any of these organisations.

Kooth A free, safe and anonymous place to find online support and counselling and share your experiences. www.kooth.com

Samaritans Confidential emotional support for anyone in emotional distress, struggling to cope or at risk of suicide. Lines open 24/7. Call free on 116 123 or visit www.samaritans.org

Childline A private and confidential service for young people up to age 19. Counsellors available to talk about anything. Call free on 0800 1111 or talk online at www.childline.org.uk

YoungMinds Mental health support for young people, including a free 24/7 crisis text-messaging service. For urgent help, text 'YM' to 85258 or visit www.youngminds.org.uk

NSPCC The UK's leading charity helping children. www.nspcc.org.uk

Mind Provides advice and support to empower anyone experiencing a mental health problem and those who care for them. Infoline 0300 123 3393 or visit www.mind.org.uk

The Mix A support service for young people going through all kinds of challenges, from mental health to money. They also provide a telephone counselling service. Visit www.themix.org.uk or @TheMixUK or call on 0808 808 4994

Stem4 Supports mental health in teenagers. Visit stem4.org.uk

Papyrus Support for young people struggling to cope with life. Visit www.papyrus-uk.org

Beat Support for people suffering with eating disorders. Visit www.beateatingdisorders.org.uk

OCD Youth Support and help for people under 25 with OCD. Visit ocdyouth.org

Alumina A free, online course for 11-19 year olds struggling with self harm. Visit selfharm.co.uk

Acknowledgements

Thank you so much to my wonderful, dear friend and editor Jenny Jacoby, who met me one sunny afternoon by the river, bought me a melty chocolate cookie and said, 'Have you ever thought of writing about writing?' Jenny – who made it all happen! Thank you for making sense of the mess.

Thank you to my agents Jodie, Molly and Emily at United.

Thank you to Lotte for the beautiful illustrations.

Thank you to Jennie Roman for the copy edit and making the words shine! Thank you to Christina Webb for the proofread.

Thank you to Louise Millar for the design and thank you to Zoe Cross or the essential read and kind words.

Thank you to my readers.

Thank you to all of the students I've ever taught – you're actually the ones who taught me. I just wasn't going to tell you that at the time. Obvs.

And a special thank you to all of the hardworking and magnificent teachers and librarians I am lucky enough to meet at school visits; those who go out of their way to book author appearances, who arrange signings, who slide into the DMs, who bake cakes and ferry authors to and from the train station in the pouring rain. Who hold book clubs, writing competitions and events, who join in on exercises with enthusiasm, who inspire and excite us, who bravely put their hand up to ask a question when the whole school hall falls silent, who laugh when nobody else laughs at our terrible author jokes, who make beautiful display boards, who don't give up, who say, 'Yes you can!' The cheerleader teachers who put grammar and spelling to one side for a minute and push for the story, for creativity and confidence. The teachers who send me little hand-written adventure stories by their students, who encourage one another to read out loud that poem they wrote about the sky. Teachers and librarians who understand that stories are everywhere, that stories bind together all of learning, all of life. Teachers and librarians who love stories so much they become completely infectious; thank you for being so generous. You are a main character in the story of a growing child's mind; you are a story! You might be really tired but PLEASE don't give up. Even if the kids forget to show their gratitude right now, they are grateful, I promise.

We see you! Thank you for all of your hard work.

Love,
Laura

Laura Dockrill

Laura Dockrill is an award-winning, critically acclaimed author. She has written and published over fifteen books for adults and children.

Laura attended The Brit School and has written since she was able to hold a pen. She writes poetry, songs and scripts too – her short film *Goldfish* being nominated for a BAFTA in 2020.

She has performed her work everywhere from Glastonbury Festival to *Blue Peter*.

Laura has taught creative writing workshops for more than ten years in and out of the UK. She runs a regular Writing Masterclass at the *Guardian*.

She lives in London with her husband, her young son and pet goldfish.